Songwriter's Rhyming Dictionary

Quick, Simple and Easy-to-Use
Rock, Pop, Folk & Hip-Hop

Jake Jackson

FLAME TREE
PUBLISHING

Publisher and Creative Director: Nick Wells
Project Editor: Catherine Taylor
Layout Design: Jake

Special thanks to: Sara Robson

10 12 14 13 11
1 3 5 7 9 10 8 6 4 2

This edition first published 2010 by
FLAME TREE PUBLISHING
Crabtree Hall, Crabtree Lane
Fulham, London SW6 6TY
United Kingdom

www.flametreepublishing.com

Flame Tree Publishing is part of
The Foundry Creative Media Co. Ltd

© 2010 this edition The Foundry Creative Media Co. Ltd

ISBN 978-1-84786-718-6

A CIP record for this book is available from the British
Library upon request.

Acknowledgments
Photographs (p18): (Jay-Z) © Paul Hebert/Icon
SMI/Corbis, (Paul Simon) © Henry Diltz/Corbis.
Other images courtesy of Foundry Arts.

Jake Jackson (author) is a musician and songwriter with a
number of music titles to his credit, including *Guitar Chords,
Piano Chords, Learn to Play Flamenco* and *Scales & Modes.*

Printed in China

How to Use this Book
The Short Version

Divided into six simple sections the *Songwriter's Rhyming Dictionary* is an essential tool for writing lyrics. The main part of the book is divided into six easy sections, organized by vowel ('a', 'e', 'i', 'o', 'u') and '**tion**' (as in 'imagination'). This is followed by a word list in alphabetical order.

So, four easy steps:

1. Work out the last-syllable sound of the word you're trying to rhyme
2. Think of the *sound* not just the *spelling* of the word
3. Search for your sound in the main sections or for your word in the word list at the back
4. Think laterally, *not* literally

Remember, your own imagination is the most important factor in your lyric. This simple guide will equip you with a battery of rhymes which can help you craft a great idea into an even greater song.

Intro

'a'

'e'

'i'

'o'

'u'

'tion'

Word List

Intro

'a'

'e'

'i'

'o'

'u'

'tion'

Word List

How to Use this Book:
The More Interesting Version

Sometimes songwriters and singers forget... They get a melody in their head and the notes will take precedence, so that they wind up forcing a word onto a melody. It doesn't ring true.

Don Henley (The Eagles)

Writing a good lyric requires craftsmanship – fitting words to rhythms and tunes, and carving them into the spaces between the beats. Inspiration is a great place to start, but finishing and polishing, and finding the right cadence in the words and the rhymes, are essential to successful songwriting.

It is not uncommon to be in a band where the lead guitarist or the drummer starkly remarks that nobody listens to the words. Any decent songwriter will quietly boil about this and it is a common source of musical differences in a band. For those of us who love the words as well as the music, we have some pretty stellar companions: Eminem, John Lennon and Paul Simon for instance, all of whose clever, emotional lyrics would hook any audience into a new world. However, it is true that some musicians and some genres do care less about the words than the construction of the melodies and the harmonies, but really, they should go and write some great instrumentals!

This book is about songs and songs need good words to communicate their complete message. As Don Henley says, the phrasing of music and verbal language have to move in sync. Most successful songs have rhymes, and this book aims to help you find that perfect series of rhymes for your idea and to provoke thought. Often the search for a rhyme provides the spark for further inspiration, firing the imagination in unexpected directions.

Language, being a living, sinuous beast, is more than just a jumble of letters; it is your own context that

'a'

'e'

'i'

'o'

'u'

'tion'

Word
List

Intro

'a'

'e'

'i'

'o'

'u'

'tion'

Word
List

releases the meaning within. That is, how the words are actually used is up to you – for example, 'fine' can be used as an adjective or verb, or adverb, the context is all. The key issue is to use the rhymes to develop thoughts and emotions, to capture the listener's interest, working hand-in-hand with the melody to create that great song.

From The Golden Age to the Age of Bling

Were it written fifty years ago, this would be a very different book. The 'Golden Age' of Tin Pan Alley songwriters had produced a generation of clean, clever, cut-glass lyrics that were as carefully constructed as the musical theatre of Oscar and Hammerstein and their ilk. But the explosive union of the blues and a generation of teenagers ready to listen to music their parents did not like created a surge of musical invention from the late 1950s and beyond. A prolonged and intense period of rock music moved the language of song into darker, tougher territory, continuing with the tempestuous

arrival of Rap, and its devil brother Hip-hop, which
burned a path into the abyss of underclass despair.
It brought the language of the street firmly onto
mainstream radio, replacing the rhythm guitar with
a rapping, fast-talking vocal, placing an even greater
emphasis on the word as the driver of the song.
Strip away the homophobia, mysogyny and the
violence that feature in the worst examples of the
genre and you find dynamic expositions of
destitution and a casual use of street language
released from the formality of written language.
Rap has its own centre of lyric gravity and this
liberates rhymes that can often only work as a
walking, talking rap. Heavy Metal, too, has its own
language, as do Pop, Folk and church and protest
songs like Joni Mitchell's 'Big Yellow Taxi'.

Some Basic Rhyming Rules

Now, back to the rhymes. This is a songwriter's
rhyming dictionary, so it is subject to a few rules

'a'

'e'

'i'

'o'

'u'

'tion'

Word
List

Intro

'a'

'e'

'i'

'o'

'u'

'tion'

Word List

which have governed the selection of words and phrases it contains, with an emphasis on words that are intended to be sung or rapped rather than read.

- No swearwords. Swearing is easy, anyone can use it, you don't need a book like this to help you. A single, carefully placed swearword can make a huge impact, but you don't need a rhyme to make it work!

- No place names, unless they are particularly iconic or resonant, such as Cannes or Beijing. Usually such choices are included because they offer a mood or a meaning beyond the obvious rhyme.

- Emphasis on the ironic. This has saved some entries, because otherwise banal words (such as 'cake', 'food', 'dryer') can be turned into something more interesting. In Hip-hop and Rap, for instance, 'respectfully request' can be spat or spoken demurely – it certainly isn't boring!

- Simple and direct is best, no formal or archaic words. It's a song, it has to be understood quickly. Even a profound song must deliver its message swiftly to the ear, so the rhymes must never get in the way. For instance 'clean slate' rhymes well with 'you hate', but 'collate' and 'oblate' have no place in this book. The same applies to some other simple rhymes which might deserve their place in great literature – 'thereby', 'thee' – but not in a modern song.

- Conversational and naturalistic language is often included, despite frequently leading to cliché. In poetry, cliché is rarely acceptable, because it no longer delivers anything new; but in a song, it arrives with a tune, a particular voice and a backing track, which together can turn the cliché on its head.

- Foreign words and phrases are generally excluded unless they are easily understood. We live in a multicultural society so there are some words and

'a'

'e'

'i'

'o'

'u'

'tion'

Word List

Intro

'a'

'e'

'i'

'o'

'u'

'tion'

Word
List

phrases which do trip off the tongue, like Paul McCartney's 'Michelle, ma belle'. It can lend the subject of the song a patina of sophistication without having to spell it out.

- Use of colloquial language. In a song the phonetic rhyme is as powerful as the perfect one, especially if the subject or the singer are using language as a signpost to the meaning of the song, such as Blur's 'Park Life'. In this context 'alright guv?' and 'kind of' become credible rhymes for that most tricky of rhyming words, 'love'.

- Potentially extensive lists of words from certain topics – such as farming or eating – have been avoided: 'ewe' and 'new' might be technically perfect but I just can't see it as a useable rhyme. Likewise, most business expressions have been excluded unless they have social, political or imaginative dimensions, so you won't find 'pie chart' as a rhyme for 'my heart'.

Following these simple rules has both reduced the vast number of potentially eligible words and expanded the range everyday phrases which can be used to extend the impact of a simple source rhymes.

Cliché or Original, Context is All

It is how you use the rhymes in the song that matters. Political and protest songs, for instance, unleash a range of social words and phrases centring on campaigning issues such as human rights, climate change, oppression and injustice. Over the decades, the songs of Woody Guthrie, Billy Bragg and The Manic Street Preachers, for instance, have brought in rhymes that would be hard to justify in any other context. Heavy Metal lyrics revel in gore and fantasy, Prog Rock fell in love with the language of mythology, Punk Rock screamed its disenchantment and despair. What can sound trite in one style of music can fit perfectly well for another. So some words lend themselves to Folk songs – think 'briar' and 'May pole' – while in Hip-hop

Intro

'a'

'e'

'i'

'o'

'u'

'tion'

Word
List

or Grunge you're more likely to need industrial and urban language. Obviously it's important to be clear about the subject and the mood of your song.

Some Useful Techniques

The rhymes in this book can be used to play with ideas, to discover, explore and challenge, so it's worth thinking about some ways of doing this:

- Rhymes don't have to appear at the end of a line. Internal or mid-line rhymes can push a song, particularly the chorus, along. Rhyming couplets can be very powerful but, if your lines are long and the music is less than bouncy, some mid-line rhymes can help keep the interest of the listener.

- The longer the rhyme, the more interesting and varied the narrative. Rhymes can be very tyrannical and demanding because they force the ear into an obvious jump from rhyme to rhyme,

but the more interesting and longer the rhyme –
and thus the more subtle – the more effective it is
in telling a story.

'a'

- Use opposites to create tension in the song. For
example, with the Smiths, you can find yourself
dancing to Morrissey's grim lyrics because they
are sugar coated by Johnny Marr's sonic bombast.
The listener's ears pick up and seek the sad words
because they contradict the music.

'e'

'i'

- Use metaphor rather than just a literal rhyme.
Rhyming 'hammer blow' with 'didn't know' offers
more interesting possibilities if it is used as a
metaphor: the words and phrases in this book
should be used like this.

'o'

'u'

- Use the banal to create unexpected resonances.
Even 'bubble wrap' can be lent sinister and
unexpected connotations if used with care. If
you're already in a creative frame of mind then

'tion'

Word
List

Intro

'a'

'e'

'i'

'o'

'u'

'tion'

Word
List

something as potentially benign as 'toy chest' can be profoundly evocative or create tension, acting as a metaphor for innocence or a Pandora's box of evil – representing the last mote of innocence in a house of abuse and violence, for instance; 'daisy chains' can turn into daisy cutters; innocent words and rhymes can be invested with deadly intent.

- The use of unusual subjects releases a new stream of language and rhymes: P. J. Harvey and Nick Cave's dark songs of countryside murder give new meaning to 'river' and 'stream', which in another context might be romantic or uplifting. Use the rhymes as a way of exploring new subjects.

- The vocabulary of darkness has greater potential than the simpler major-key directness of pop songs. This is not intended as a value judgment, it is simply a fact that the melancholy and the cynical provide a wider range of emotions and experience, which unlocks a huge number of effective and interesting rhymes.

Lyrics in a Digital Age

Rhymes are subject to fashion and change, and play their part in the reflection of our society, its preoccupations and seductions (indeed, fashion and trends inevitably play some part in the reasons for inclusion in, or exclusion from, this book). Technology has moved swiftly from long-playing records, through a brief flirtation with CDs, to the full onslaught of digital downloads and online video. Lyrics are often left behind in the struggle to find an audience, with some of the information provided with songs barely managing to present reliable songwriter credits. But lyrics are powerful tools: people sing them, study them and admire them, and I hope this book will help you to explore, discover and scale the heights of your own songwriting challenges.

Intro

'a'

'e'

'i'

'o'

'u'

'tion'

Word
List

A Note on Pronunciation

There are some significant differences in pronunciation between the US and UK (manifested strikingly in names like 'Van Gogh'). Much of the language of music is transatlantic, so a wider range of phonetic rhymes is potentially available for this reason, enabling, for instance, 'clock' to rhyme with 'walk' even if the singer's native accent is British (since singers are not bound by their speaking accent when singing). Moreover, there are significant regional variations in accent within all so-called English language countries and cultures. It is important to be aware of the opportunities offered by the different pronunciation of words, without sacrificing credibility. Frequently in this book, words with different possible pronunciations are placed under each relevant vowel sound.

A List of Great Lyricists

Make a point of listening to the rhymes and techniques in the songs of these great artists. This is not an exhaustive list but offers a fair range. You can join a discussion about the best lyricists on the Flame Tree Music page on Facebook. facebook

Gary Barlow (Take That), 'Another Crack in the Heart'

David Byrne, 'Psycho Killer'

Sammy Cahn, 'Three Coins in the Fountain'

Nick Cave, 'Breathless'

Johnny Cash, 'Unchained'

Eric Clapton, 'Tears in Heaven'

Elvis Costello, 'Oliver's Army'

Leonard Cohen, 'Hallelujah'

Jarvis Cocker, 'Common People'

Ian Dury (and The Blockheads), 'Billericay Dickie'

Bob Dylan, 'All Along the Watchtower'

Ray Davies (The Kinks), 'Waterloo Sunset'

Eminem, 'Lose Yourself'

Intro

'a'

'e'

'i'

'o'

'u'

'tion'

Word
List

Jay-Z

Woody Guthrie, 'Christ for President'

Jay-Z, 'Empire State of Mind'

Carole King, 'Jazzman'

John Lennon, 'Imagine'

Lennon/McCartney, 'Yesterday'

Bob Marley, 'Babylon System'

Paul McCartney, 'Jet'

Morrissey (The Smiths), 'Half a Person'

Joni Mitchell, 'Big Yellow Taxi'

Cole Porter, 'Anything Goes'

Rakim, 'After You Die'

Lou Reed, 'Walk on The Wild Side'

Robbie Robertson, 'Fallen Angel'

Mike Rutherford (Mike + the Mechanics), 'Living Years'

Paul Simon, '50 Ways to Leave Your Lover'

Tupac Shakur, 'A Day in the Life'

Patti Smith, 'Free Money'

Bruce Springsteen, 'Tunnel of Love'

Cat Stevens, 'Miles From Nowhere'

Tom Waits, 'House Where Nobody Lives'

Alex Turner (Arctic Monkeys), 'Mardy Bum'

Richard Thompson, 'Persuasion'

Roger Waters, 'The Tide is Turning'

Thom Yorke, 'All for the Best'

'a'

'e'

'i'

'o'

'u'

'tion'

Word
List

Paul Simon

Intro

'a'

'e'

'i'

'o'

'u'

'tion'

Word List

...ab
(e.g. grab)

1 Syllable

blab, cab, crab, drab, fab, flab, gab, grab, jab, lab,
nab, scab, slab, stab, tab

2 Syllables

prefab, don't blab

3 Syllables

chemistry lab, lookin' fab, taxi cab

4 Syllables

gift of the gab

...abe
(e.g. babe)

1 Syllable
babe

2 Syllables
my babe

3 Syllables
you're my babe

4 Syllables
I got you babe

Intro

'a'

'e'

'i'

'o'

'u'

'tion'

Word
List

...ace

(e.g. face)

1 Syllable

ace, base, bass, brace, case, chase, face, grace, lace, mace, pace, place, race, space, trace, vase

2 Syllables

air base, apace, arms race, blank space, car race, debase, deep space, deface, disc space, disgrace, disk space, displace, efface, embrace, erase, first base, gun case, horse race, in case, misplace, neck brace, rat race, replace, retrace, sack race, shoe lace, take place, touch base

3 Syllables

army base, breathing space, display case, enclosed space, hiding place, holy place, human race, interlace, just in case, living space, master race, meeting place, navy base, nesting place, outer space, out of place, packing case, paper chase, parking space, pencil case, relay race, state of grace, stay in place, storage space, trophy case, upper case

4 Syllables

attaché case, cigarette case, custody case, fall into place, gathering pace, in any case, in the first place, memory trace, obstacle race, overnight case, visual space

5 Syllables

interstellar space

6 Syllables

imaginary place

Intro

'a'

'e'

'i'

'o'

'u'

'tion'

Word List

'a'

...aced

(e.g. raced)

see page 73 ...aste (e.g. waste)

...ack

(e.g. back)

1 Syllable

back, black, crack, flack, hack, jack, knack, lack, mac,
pack, plaque, quack, rack, sac, sack, shack, slack,
smack, snack, stack, tack, track, wack, whack,
wrack, yack, yak

2 Syllables

attack, coal black, dirt track, half track, ice pack, jet
black, knick-knack, phone jack, pitch black, sad sack,
tie rack, unpack, wolf pack

3 Syllables

air attack, heart attack, hit the sack, inside track,
jumping jack, luggage rack, power pack, railroad
track, union jack

4 Syllables

ivory black, panic attack, plan of attack, surprise
attack, telephone jack, under attack

5 Syllables

off the beaten track, political hack

Intro

'a'

'e'

'i'

'o'

'u'

'tion'

Word
List

Intro

'a'

'e'

'i'

'o'

'u'

'tion'

Word
List

...act

(e.g. act)

1 Syllable

act, backed, blacked, cracked, fact, hacked, jacked,
lacked, packed, pact, racked, sacked, slacked,
smacked, snacked, stacked, tacked, tact, tracked,
tract, whacked, wracked

2 Syllables

abstract, attacked, attract, compact, contract,
distract, enact, exact, extract, impact, intact, in fact,
react, retract, subtract, unpacked

3 Syllables

interact

4 Syllables

counterattacked, in point of fact, matter of fact,

overreact, suicide pact

6 Syllables

as a matter of fact

8 Syllables

accessory after the fact

...ad

(e.g. glad)

1 Syllable

ad, add, bad, cad, clad, dad, fad, glad, had, lad,

mad, pad, plaid, sad

Intro

'a'

'e'

'i'

'o'

'u'

'tion'

Word List

2 Syllables

forbad, launch pad, like mad, not bad, too bad

3 Syllables

raving mad, shoulder pad, writing pad

4 Syllables

newspaper ad

...ade
(e.g. trade)

1 Syllable

ade, aid, aide, bade, bayed, blade, braid, fade, flayed,
frayed, glade, grade, jade, laid, made, maid, paid, played,
prayed, preyed, raid, shade, spade, sprayed, staid, stayed,
strayed, suede, swayed, they'd, trade, wade, weighed

2 Syllables

afraid, air raid, allayed, arcade, arrayed, band aid,
betrayed, blockade, brigade, brocade, cascade,
charade, clichéd, conveyed, crusade, decade, decayed,
degrade, delayed, dismayed, displayed, dissuade,
downgrade, evade, fan blade, first aid, first grade,
forbade, get laid, grenade, handmade, homemade,
invade, knife blade, lamp shade, manmade, mislaid,
obeyed, outweighed, parade, persuade, portrayed,
prepaid, remade, repaid, replayed, surveyed, tirade,
unmade, unpaid, unswayed, upgrade

3 Syllables

disobeyed, hand grenade, hearing aid, lemonade,
masquerade, overpaid, overplayed, overstayed, rotor
blade, serenade, shoulder blade, smoke grenade,
unafraid, underpaid, underplayed, window shade,
wiper blade

4 Syllables

financial aid, fire brigade, penny arcade

Intro

'a'

'e'

'i'

'o'

'u'

'tion'

Word List

6 Syllables
military blockade

7 Syllables
audiovisual aid

...aff
(e.g. calf)

1 Syllable
barf, calf, graph, half, laugh, scarf, staff

2 Syllables
behalf, giraffe

3 Syllables
chief of staff, golden calf, office staff

Intro

'a'

'e'

'i'

'o'

'u'

'tion'

Word List

4 Syllables

general staff

...aff

(e.g. gaffe)

1 Syllable

gaff, gaffe, graph, staff

2 Syllables

carafe, giraffe

3 Syllables

chief of staff, office staff

4 Syllables

general staff

Intro

"a"

"e"

"i"

"o"

"u"

'tion'

Word List

...ag

(e.g. rag)

1 Syllable

bag, blagg, brag, drag, fag, flag, gag, hag, lag, mag,

nag, rag, sag, shag, slag, snag, stag, tag, wag

2 Syllables

jet lag, kit bag, old bag, price tag, time lag

3 Syllables

paper bag, pirate flag, sleeping bag, union flag

4 Syllables

national flag, overnight bag

...age

(e.g. rage)

1 Syllable

age, cage, gage, gauge, page, rage, sage, stage, wage

2 Syllables

assuage, engage, enrage, offstage, of age, old age, onstage, rib cage, space age, stone age, upstage

3 Syllables

come of age, disengage, fuel gauge, golden age, take the stage, underage

4 Syllables

minimum wage

Intro

'a'

'e'

'i'

'o'

'u'

'tion'

Word
List

...ain
(e.g. pain)

1 Syllable

bane, brain, cane, chain, crane, drain, feign, gain,
grain, lain, lane, main, mane, pain, pane, plain, plane,
rain, reign, rein, sane, slain, Spain, sprain, stain,
strain, train, vain, vane, vein, wane

2 Syllables

abstain, again, arcane, attain, campaign, champagne,
cocaine, complain, constrain, contain, detain, disdain,
domain, explain, fast lane, food chain, free rein,
freight train, gas main, humane, inane, insane, in
vain, jet plane, left brain, maintain, mundane, obtain,
oil stain, profane, pull chain, refrain, regain, remain,
restrain, retain, retrain, right brain, slow lane,
sustain, terrain, urbane

3 Syllables

acid rain, ad campaign, ascertain, ball and chain,
daisy chain, entertain, express train, gravy train,
inhumane, in the main, mental strain, nervous strain,
overtrain, subway train, sugar cane, take in vain,
wagon train, weather vane

4 Syllables

capital gain, commuter train, financial gain, jugular
vein, public domain

5 Syllables

whispering campaign

6 Syllables

advertising campaign, military campaign,
political campaign

Intro

'a'

'e'

'i'

'o'

'u'

'tion'

Word
List

...air

(e.g. hair)

1 Syllable

air, bare, bear, blare, care, chair, dare, fair, fare, flair, flare, glare, hair, lair, mare, pair, pear, prayer, rare, scare, share, snare, spare, square, stair, stare, swear, tear, their, there, ware, wear, where

2 Syllables

affair, au pair, aware, beware, bus fare, cab fare, compare, cross hair, deckchair, declare, despair, ensnare, great bear, hot air, ice bear, impair, lord's prayer, mid-air, prepare, repair, take care, Times Square, unfair

3 Syllables

billionaire, evening prayer, grizzly bear, laissez faire, love affair, millionaire, morning prayer, open air, polar bear, premiere, questionnaire, subway fare, taxi fare, teddy bear, unaware, wear and tear

4 Syllables

out of thin air, up in the air, walking on air,
world premiere

...aint
(e.g. faint)

1 Syllable

ain't, faint, feignt, feint, paint, quaint, saint, taint

2 Syllables

acquaint, complaint, constraint, oil paint, repaint,
restraint, war paint

Intro

'a'

'e'

'i'

'o'

'u'

'tion'

Word
List

...ake
(e.g. shake)

1 Syllable

ache, bake, brake, break, cake, fake, flake, lake, make, quake, rake, sake, shake, slake, snake, stake, steak, take, wake

2 Syllables

awake, foot brake, forsake, hand brake, head ache, hot cake, mistake, opaque, partake, to make

3 Syllables

angel cake, chocolate cake, minute steak, piece of cake, stomach ache, wedding cake

4 Syllables

angel food cake, devil's food cake, hydraulic brake

5 Syllables

artificial lake, emergency brake

...ale
(e.g. pale)

1 Syllable

ail, ale, bail, bale, braille, dale, fail, flail, frail, gale, grail, hail, jail, mail, male, nail, pail, pale, rail, sail, sale, scale, shale, snail, stale, tail, tale, they'll, trail, vale, veil, wail, whale

2 Syllables

air mail, assail, avail, blue whale, chain mail, curtail, derail, detail, email, entail, exhale, forced sale, for sale, hay bale, inhale, prevail, sperm whale, surveil, tall tale, turn tail, unveil, white whale, wind scale

3 Syllables

bill of sale, cattle trail, clearance sale, coat of mail, fire sale, ginger ale, holy grail, humpback whale, jumble sale, mountain trail, old wives' tale, picture rail, richter scale, rummage sale, safety rail, sliding scale

Intro
'a'
'e'
'i'
'o'
'u'
'tion'
Word List

Intro

'a'

'e'

'i'

'o'

'u'

'tion'

Word
List

4 Syllables

heroic tale, indian trail

5 Syllables

electronic mail

6 Syllables

economies of scale

...alk

(e.g. walk)

1 Syllable

balk, chalk, clock, cork, dork, fork, gawk, hawk, pork,

squawk, stalk, stork, talk, walk

2 Syllables

ad-hoc, crosstalk, shop talk, small talk, sweet talk

3 Syllables

baby talk, double talk, empty talk, flower stalk,

idle talk

...all

(e.g. wall)

1 Syllable

all, ball, bawl, brawl, call, crawl, drawl, fall, gall, Gaul,
hall, haul, mall, maul, pall, scrawl, shawl, small, spall,
sprawl, squall, stall, tall, thrall, wall

Intro

'a'

'e'

'i'

'o'

'u'

'tion'

Word List

Intro

'a'

'e'

'i'

'o'

'u'

'tion'

Word List

2 Syllables

appall, at all, befall, close call, crank call, curved ball,
dance hall, install, in all, long haul, masked ball, no ball,
phone call, prayer shawl, pub crawl, recall, trunk call

3 Syllables

above all, all in all, collect call, concert hall, cricket
ball, curtain call, first of all, music hall, on the ball,
shopping mall, tennis ball, urban sprawl

4 Syllables

once and for all, telephone call

...alt
(e.g. halt)

1 Syllable
fault, halt, malt, salt, vault

2 Syllables
assault, at fault, default, exalt, find fault, old salt

3 Syllables
to a fault

4 Syllables
burial vault

5 Syllables
San Andreas fault, sexual assault

Intro

'a'

'e'

'i'

'o'

'u'

'tion'

Word
List

'a'

...alve
(e.g. halve)

see page 68 ...arve (e.g. carve)

...alve
(e.g. salve)

1 Syllable
salve, valve

2 Syllables
lipsalve, bivalve

...am

(e.g. slam)

1 Syllable

am, bam, clam, cram, dam, damn, *femme*, gram,
ham, jam, lamb, ma'am, 'nam, ram, R.A.M., scam,
sham, slam, spam, swam, wham

2 Syllables

exam, grand slam, madame

3 Syllables

give a damn, rack of lamb, traffic jam, uncle sam

4 Syllables

battering ram, final exam, oral exam,
strawberry jam

Intro

'a'

'e'

'i'

'o'

'u'

'tion'

Word List

Intro

"a"

"e"

"i"

"o"

"u"

'tion'

Word List

...ame

(e.g. name)

1 Syllable

aim, blame, came, claim, dame, fame, flame, frame, game, lame, maim, name, same, shame, tame

2 Syllables

acclaim, aflame, ashame, ballgame, ball game, became, big game, card game, chess game, declaim, defame, disclaim, exclaim, fair game, grande dame, head game, home game, ill fame, inflame, lay claim, night game, pay claim, proclaim, reclaim, rename, road game, shell game, take aim, the same, war game, word game

3 Syllables

all the same, away game, bloody shame, candle flame, guessing game, hall of fame, laying claim, numbers game, open frame, outdoor game, overcame, parlo(u)r game, party game, passing game, perfect game,

Intro

'a'

'e'

'i'

'o'

'u'

'tion'

Word List

picture frame, poker game, sense of shame, set aflame,
table game, waiting game, window frame, without aim

4 Syllables

computer game, insurance claim, one and the same,
video game

...amp

(e.g. lamp)

1 Syllable

amp, camp, champ, clamp, cramp, damp, lamp,
stamp, tramp, vamp

2 Syllables

break camp, date stamp, food stamp, revamp,

3 Syllables

prison camp, rubber stamp, summer camp, writer's cramp

Intro

'a'

'e'

'i'

'o'

'u'

'tion'

Word
List

...an

(e.g. ran)

1 Syllable

an, ban, Cannes, clan, fan, flan, gran, man, nan, pan,
plan, ran, scan, span, tan, than, van

2 Syllables

beer can, began, best man, blind man, cave man, con
man, front man, game plan, ground plan, hit man,
old man, poor man, rich man, sedan, sports fan, spray
can, straw man, stunt man, tin can, trash can, wild
man, wise man, young man, you can

3 Syllables

common man, fancy man, frying pan, garbage can,
garbage man, hatchet man, holy man, ladies' man,
married man, master plan, minivan, modern man,
muffin man, overran, police van, preacher man,
secret plan, soda can, wealthy man, working man

4 Syllables

attention span, company man, electric fan, family man, gingerbread man, maintenance man, medicine man, miracle man, unmarried man

5 Syllables

delivery van, military man, neanderthal man

...ance

(e.g. dance)

1 Syllable

chance, dance, france, glance, stance, trance

2 Syllables

advance, askance, by chance, enhance, expanse, finance, romance

Intro

'a'

'e'

'i'

'o'

'u'

'tion'

Word List

Intro

'a'

'e'

'i'

'o'

'u'

'tion'

Word
List

3 Syllables

at first glance, cash advance, even chance,
game of chance, happy chance, high finance,
in advance, take a chance

4 Syllables

hypnotic trance, religious trance

...and
(e.g. hand)

1 Syllable

and, band, banned, bland, brand, canned, fanned,
gland, grand, hand, land, manned, panned, planned,
sand, scanned, spanned, stand, strand, tanned

2 Syllables

arm band, big band, brake band, brass band,

command, crash land, dance band, dead hand,
demand, disband, dry land, expand, firsthand, jazz
band, offhand, on land, outmanned, remand,
righthand, rock band, steel band, unmanned,
unplanned, whip hand, withstand

3 Syllables

common land, cash in hand, close at hand, helping
hand, high command, hired hand, holy land, minute
hand, native land, no man's land, out of hand,
promised land, rubber band, second hand, sleight of
hand, take the stand, understand, upper hand,
wedding band, witness stand

4 Syllables

misunderstand, take a firm stand

5 Syllables

cultivated land, military band,
on the other hand

Intro

'a'

'e'

'i'

'o'

'u'

'tion'

Word
List

Intro

'a'

'e'

'i'

'o'

'u'

'tion'

Word List

...ane

(e.g. wane)

see page 36 ... ain (e.g. pain)

...ang

(e.g. rang)

1 Syllable

bang, clang, fang, gang, hang, rang, sang, slang, spang, sprang

2 Syllables

chain gang, harangue, press gang

3 Syllables

Sturm und Drang

...ank
(e.g. blank)

1 Syllable

bank, blank, clank, crank, dank, drank, flank, frank, plank, prank, rank, sank, shank, shrank, spank, stank, swank, tank, thank, yank

2 Syllables

blood bank

3 Syllables

antitank, central bank

5 Syllables

military rank

Intro

'a'

'e'

'i'

'o'

'u'

'tion'

Word List

Intro

'a'

'e'

'i'

'o'

'u'

'tion'

Word
List

...ap
(e.g. cap)

1 Syllable

app, cap, chap, clap, crap, flap, gap, lap, map,

nap, rap, sap, scrap, slap, snap, strap, tap, trap,

wrap, yap, zap

2 Syllables

chin strap, cold snap, entrap, gift wrap, recap, sand

trap, speed trap, unwrap

3 Syllables

booby trap, bubble wrap, water gap, water tap,

weather map

...ape
(e.g. shape)

1 Syllable

ape, cape, drape, gape, grape, rape, scape, scrape,
shape, tape

2 Syllables

escape, great ape, red tape, reshape

3 Syllables

ticker tape

4 Syllables

fire escape, magnetic tape, narrow escape, videotape

Intro

'a'

'e'

'i'

'o'

'u'

'tion'

Word List

...apt
(e.g. capped)

1 Syllable

apt, capped, clapped, flapped, lapped, mapped, napped, rapped, rapt, sapped, scrapped, slapped, snapped, strapped, tapped, trapped, wrapped, zapped

2 Syllables

adapt, entrapped, inept, recapped, untapped, unwrapped

...ar
(e.g. far)

1 Syllable

are, bar, car, far, jar, mar, par, sar, scar, star

2 Syllables

afar, ajar, bazaar, bell jar, bizarre, cigar, coal tar, dog star, film star, freight car, guitar, North Star, rock star, snack bar, space bar, sports car, squad car, you are

3 Syllables

cable car, candy bar, chocolate bar, cookie jar, morning star, movie star, polar star, police car, racing car, railroad car, railway car, shooting star, steel guitar, superstar, tv star

4 Syllables

passenger car

Intro

'a'

'e'

'i'

'o'

'u'

'tion'

Word
List

Intro

'a'

'e'

'i'

'o'

'u'

'tion'

Word List

...arce

(e.g. farce)

1 Syllable

arse, brass, class, crass, farce, glass, grass, parse, pass, sparse

2 Syllables

beer glass, cut glass, first class, forecast, stained glass, surpass, world class

3 Syllables

hourglass, looking glass, lower class, middle class, outclass, ruling class, second class, social class, trespass, upper class, working class

4 Syllables

pain in the arse

...ard
(e.g. card)

1 Syllable

bard, card, charred, guard, hard, lard, marred,
scarred, shard, sparred, starred, tarred, yard

2 Syllables

bombard, die hard, discard, *en garde*, off guard, old
guard, on guard, regard, retard, stand guard,
strike hard

3 Syllables

avant-garde, bodyguard, disregard, off your guard,
on your guard, prison guard, railway yard,
scotland yard

Intro

'a'

'e'

'i'

'o'

'u'

'tion'

Word
List

...are
(e.g. care)

see page 38 ...air (e.g. hair)

...ark
(e.g. spark)

1 Syllable

arc, ark, bark, clerk, dark, lark, mark, park, shark, spark, stark

2 Syllables

bank clerk, bench mark, burn mark, car park, desk clerk, embark, remark, stretch mark, white shark

3 Syllables

central park, disembark, question mark, trailer park

4 Syllables

amusement park, wide of the mark

...arm

(e.g. warm)

see page 228 ...orm (e.g. form)

Intro

'a'

'e'

'i'

'o'

'u'

'tion'

Word
List

Intro

'a'

'e'

'i'

'o'

'u'

'tion'

Word
List

...arm
(e.g. harm)

1 Syllable

arm, balm, bomb, charm, farm, harm, ma'am,
mom, palm

2 Syllables

alarm, disarm, forearm, rearm, unarm

3 Syllables

funny farm, good luck charm, smoke alarm,
underarm

4 Syllables

burglar alarm, fire alarm

...arp
(e.g. sharp)

1 Syllable

carp, harp, sharp, tarp

2 Syllables

mouth harp

Intro

'a'

'e'

'i'

'o'

'u'

'tion'

Word List

Intro

'a'

'e'

'i'

'o'

'u'

'tion'

Word List

...ars

(e.g. stars)

see also page 60 ...arce
(e.g. farce) for similar rhymes

1 Syllable

bars, cars, mars, scars, stars, vase

2 Syllables

bazaars, cigars, guitars, ours

3 Syllables

behind bars, minicars, stars and bars, superstars

4 Syllables

parallel bars

...art
(e.g. heart)

1 Syllable
art, cart, chart, dart, fart, hart, heart, mart, part,
smart, start, tart

2 Syllables
apart, bit part, depart, fresh start, head start, impart,
kick start, restart, spare part, star chart, take heart,
take part, weak part

3 Syllables
à la carte, abstract art, bleeding heart, body part,
break apart, fall apart, set apart, take apart, take to
heart, tear apart, tease apart, tell apart

4 Syllables
for the most part, state of the art, taken apart

Intro

'a'

'e'

'i'

'o'

'u'

'tion'

Word
List

...arve

(e.g. carve)

1 Syllable

carve, halve, starve

...ash

(e.g. ash)

1 Syllable

ash, bash, brash, cache, cash, clash, crash, dash, flash,
gash, gnash, hash, lash, mash, rash, sash, slash,
smash, splash, stash, tash, thrash, trash

2 Syllables

heat rash, hot flush, panache, rehash, white trash

Intro

'a'

'e'

'i'

'o'

'u'

'tion'

Word List

3 Syllables

diaper rash, in a flash, nettle rash, petty cash,
window sash

4 Syllables

memory cache

...ash
(e.g. wash)

1 Syllable

gosh, josh, posh, quash, slosh, squash, wash

2 Syllables

awash, backwash, brainwash, carwash, dry wash,
kibosh, whitewash

Intro

'a'

'e'

'i'

'o'

'u'

'tion'

Word List

...ask
(e.g. task)

1 Syllable
bask, cask, flask, mask, task, trask

2 Syllables
death mask, unmask

4 Syllables
oxygen mask

...ass
(e.g. parse)

see page 60 ...arce (e.g. farce)

70

...ass

(e.g. crass)

1 Syllable

ass, bass, brass, class, crass, gas, glass, grass, lass,
mass, pass, sass

2 Syllables

alas, amass, beer glass, crevasse, cut glass, en masse,
first class, forecasts, harass, hourglass, impasse,
jackass, outclass, stained glass, surpass, world class

3 Syllables

looking glass, lower class, middle class, ruling class,
second class, social class, trespass, upper class,
working class

4 Syllables

critical mass, pain in the ass

...ast

(e.g. past)

1 Syllable

blast, cast, caste, classed, fast, glassed, grassed, last,
massed, mast, passed, past, vast

2 Syllables

aghast, amassed, at last, bomb blast, contrast,
forecast, harassed, hold fast, miscast, outlast, recast,
sand cast, stand fast, surpassed, the last

3 Syllables

at long last, first and last, plaster cast, unsurpassed,
very fast

...aste

(e.g. waste)

1 Syllable

aced, based, braced, chased, chaste, faced, graced,
haste, laced, paced, paste, placed, raced, spaced,
taste, traced, waist, waste

2 Syllables

change taste, debased, defaced, disgraced, displaced,
distaste, embraced, encased, erased, foretaste, in
haste, misplaced, replaced

3 Syllables

interlaced, in good taste, in poor taste, sense of taste

Intro

'a'

'e'

'i'

'o'

'u'

'tion'

Word
List

...at
(e.g. hat)

1 Syllable

at, bat, brat, cat, chat, fat, flat, gnat, hat, mat, matt, pat, pratt, rat, sat, slat, spat, splat, stat, tat, that, vat

2 Syllables

and that, bath mat, begat, chip at, combat, does that, down pat, eat at, fall flat, fruit bat, get at, gnaw at, house cat, in that, is that, laugh at, look at, manx cat, mud flat, nonfat, of that, on that, pack rat, peck at, pick at, place mat, play at, pluck at, poke at, prayer mat, shine at, shop at, snap at, stay at, such that, to that, wink at, with that, work at

3 Syllables

alley cat, arrive at, a look at, baseball bat, become flat, bridle at, bristle at, connive at, cricket bat, desert rat, excel at, jungle cat, looking at, rat-a-tat, sewer rat, tabby cat, tit for tat, vampire bat, water rat, welcome mat

...atch

(e.g. catch)

1 Syllable

batch, catch, hatch, latch, match, patch, scratch, snatch, thatch

2 Syllables

attach, detach, dispatch, love match, mismatch, rematch

3 Syllables

boxing match, escape hatch, reattach, safety match, sparring match, unattach, wrestling match

4 Syllables

vegetable patch

Intro

'a'

'e'

'i'

'o'

'u'

'tion'

Word List

Intro

'a'

'e'

'i'

'o'

'u'

'tion'

Word List

...ate

(e.g. late)

1 Syllable

ate, bait, bate, crate, date, eight, fate, fete, freight, gait, gate, grate, great, hate, late, mate, pate, plate, rate, sate, skate, slate, spate, state, straight, strait, trait, wait, weight

2 Syllables

berate, birth rate, blind date, clean slate, create, crime rate, debate, deflate, dictate, dilate, elate, equate, gold plate, growth rate, heart rate, hot plate, ice skate, inflate, irate, lightweight, lose weight, ornate, relate, restate, sedate, soul mate, steel plate, tail gate, to date, translate, update, upstate

3 Syllables

armo(u)r plate, body weight, desecrate, estimate, figure skate, Golden Gate, interstate, license plate, lie in wait, overweight, solid-state, tolerate

4 Syllables

at any rate, figure of eight, interrelate, lying in wait,
pieces of eight, recriminate

5 Syllables

unemployment rate

...ath
(e.g. bath)

1 Syllable

bath, hearth, path

2 Syllables

birdbath, bloodbath, footpath,
towpath, warpath

Intro

'a'

'e'

'i'

'o'

'u'

'tion'

Word
List

Intro

'a'

'e'

'i'

'o'

'u'

'tion'

Word
List

...athe
(e.g. bathe)

1 Syllable
bathe, lathe, swathe

...augh
(e.g. laugh)

see page 32 ...aff (e.g. calf)

...ave
(e.g. wave)

1 Syllable

brave, cave, crave, gave, grave, knave, nave, pave, rave, save, shave, slave, stave, they've, waive, wave

2 Syllables

air wave, behave, brain wave, close shave, crime wave, deprave, enslave, forgave, heat wave, new wave, shortwave, short wave, sound wave

3 Syllables

misbehave, tidal wave

4 Syllables

radio wave

'a'

...ave
(e.g. have)

1 Syllable
chav, have

3 Syllables
gotta have, have to have

...aw
(e.g. saw)

see also page 271 ...ure
(e.g. pure)

1 Syllable
awe, boar, boor, bore, chore, claw, core, corps, craw,

door, draw, drawer, flaw, floor, for, fore, four, gnaw,

gore, jaw, law, lore, moor, more, oar, or, ore, paw, poor, pore, pour, raw, roar, saw, score, shore, snore, soar, sore, spore, store, straw, sure, swore, thaw, tore, tour, war, whore, wore, your

2 Syllables

abhor, adore, assure, before, bonjour, car door, class war, cold war, dance floor, decor, deplore, detour, ensure, explore, for sure, galore, grand tour, hardcore, ignore, implore, insure, make sure, next door, no more, once more, on tour, rapport, restore, señor, shop floor, side door, stage door, swing door, that you're, trap door, unsure, what for, withdraw, what you're, world war

3 Syllables

anymore, go to war, know the score, martial law, more and more, open door, reassure, state of war, take the floor, to be sure, tragic flaw

5 Syllables

prisoner of war, responsible for

Intro

'a'

'e'

'i'

'o'

'u'

'tion'

Word List

...ax

(e.g. wax)

1 Syllable

acts, axe, backs, cracks, facts, fax, hacks, jacks, knacks,
lacks, lax, macs, Macs, max, packs, pacts, plaques,
quacks, racks, sacks, sax, shacks, slacks, smacks,
snacks, stacks, tacks, tax, tracks, wax, whacks

2 Syllables

attacks, impacts, relax

...ay

(e.g. say)

Intro

'a'

'e'

'i'

'o'

'u'

'tion'

Word List

1 Syllable

bay, bray, clay, day, eh, fey, flay, fray, gay, gray,
grey, hay, hey, lay, may, pay, play, pray, prey, ray, slay,
sleigh, spray, stay, stray, sway, they, tray, way,
weigh, whey, yay

2 Syllables

and they, array, ash gray, astray, away, ballet,
betray, bouquet, buffet, café, child's play, cliché,
convey, decay, delay, dismay, display, each day, essay,
fast day, field day, filet, fine spray, foul play, give way,
hair spray, halfway, hold sway, hooray, make way,
monet, obey, okay, portray, repay, replay, school day,
sea spray, sick pay, soiree, survey, today, valet,
word play, x ray

3 Syllables

a.k.a., back away, bird of prey, break away, break of
day, by the way, C.I.A., cabaret, cast away, day by day,
die away, disarray, disobey, everyday, fade away, fall
away, faraway, file away, get away, give away, haul
away, hell to pay, judgement day, lead astray, market
day, milky way, new year's day, on the way, overplay,
overstay, point the way, potter's clay, power play, pull
away, push away, put away, rainy day, right away,
run away, shadow play, slip away, sneak away, sweep
away, take away, tear away, the whole way, throw
away, time of day, turn away, underpay, underplay,
underway, U.S.A., washing day, wash away, wear
away, wedding day, what are they, while away,
wipe away, working day

4 Syllables

breaking away, break of the day, day after day, fading
away, far and away, running away, valentine's day,
wasting away, without delay

5 Syllables

dwindling away, every which way, independence day

6 Syllables

forever and a day

...aze
(e.g. raze)

1 Syllable

blaze, bays, days, maze, phase, praise, raise,

raze, ways

2 Syllables

ablaze, allays, always, amaze, appraise betrays

3 Syllables

bygone days, full of praise, holidays

Intro

'a'

'e'

'i'

'o'

'u'

'tion'

Word List

Intro

'a'

'e'

'i'

'o'

'u'

'tion'

Word List

Intro

'a'

'e'

'i'

'o'

'u'

'tion'

Word List

Intro

'a'

'e'

'i'

'o'

'u'

'tion'

Word
List

...e

(e.g. 'baby')

see page 105 ...ee (e.g. see)

...eace

(e.g. peace)

1 Syllable

cease, crease, feasts, fleece, geese, grease, Greece,

lease, Nice, niece, piece, priests

2 Syllables

at peace, decease, decrease, increase, make peace,

obese, police, release, set piece

Intro

'a'

'e'

'i'

'o'

'u'

'tion'

Word List

3 Syllables

elbow grease, piece by piece

4 Syllables

breach of the peace, secret police

...each

(e.g. reach)

1 Syllable

beach, bleach, each, leech, peach, preach, screech, speech, teach

2 Syllables

impeach, Long Beach

Intro

'a'

'e'

'i'

'o'

'u'

'tion'

Word List

3 Syllables

one for each

4 Syllables

figure of speech, freedom of speech

5 Syllables

material breach

...ead

(e.g. mead)

see page 108 ...eed (e.g. speed)

...ead
(e.g. head)

see page 104 ...ed (e.g. led)

...ealth
(e.g. health)

1 Syllable
health, stealth, wealth

4 Syllables
drink to your health

Intro

'a'

'e'

'i'

'o'

'u'

'tion'

Word List

Intro

'a'

'e'

'i'

'o'

'u'

'tion'

Word List

...eam
(e.g. dream)

1 Syllable

beam, cream, deem, dream, gleam, ream,
scheme, scream, seam, seem, steam, stream,
team, teem, theme

2 Syllables

downstream, esteem, extreme, face cream,
Gulf stream, ice cream, jet stream, redeem,
regime, supreme, upstream

3 Syllables

coffee cream, colo(u)r scheme, laser beam

...ean

(e.g. mean)

see page 112 ...een (e.g. seen)

...ear

(e.g. fear)

1 Syllable

beer, cheer, clear, dear, deer, ear, fear, gear, hear, here, jeer, leer, mere, near, peer, pier, rear, sear, shear, sheer, smear, sneer, spear, sphere, steer, tear, veer, we're, year

2 Syllables

adhere, all clear, appear, austere, career, cashier, come near, draw near, each year, frontier, held dear, high gear, hold dear, leap year, light year, low gear,

Intro

'a'

'e'

'i'

'o'

'u'

'tion'

Word List

Intro

'a'

'e'

'i'

'o'

'u'

'tion'

Word List

per year, premiere, revere, root beer, severe, sincere, small beer, unclear, up here, veneer

3 Syllables

bend your ear, bombardier, cavalier, chandelier, commandeer, crystal clear, darkest fear, disappear, domineer, engineer, far and near, fiscal year, fishing gear, ginger beer, golden sphere, gondolier, holy year, inner ear, insincere, interfere, in one ear, last frontier, overhear, over here, persevere, pioneer, profiteer, racketeer, reappear, solar year, souvenir, world premiere

4 Syllables

every year, imagineer, reengineer

5 Syllables

bioengineer, cauliflower ear

6 Syllables

astronomical year

...ear

(e.g. wear)

see page 38 ...air (e.g. hair)

...eared

(e.g. feared)

1 Syllable

beard, cheered, cleared, eared, feared, qeared, jeered,
neared, peered, reared, seared, sheared, smeared,
sneered, steered, veered, wierd

2 Syllables

adhered, appeared, cashiered, premiered, revered

Intro

'a'

'e'

'i'

'o'

'u'

'tion'

Word List

Intro

'a'

3 Syllables

commandeered, disappeared, goatee beard,

interfered, persevered, pioneered, reappeared,

volunteered

'e'

'i'

...earn

(e.g. yearn)

see page 275 ...urn (e.g. burn)

'o'

'u'

'tion'

Word List

...ease

(e.g. tease)

1 Syllable

bees, breeze, cheese, ease, fees, fleas, freeze, frieze, keys, knees, peas, please, seas, sees, seize, sleaze, sneeze, squeeze, tease, these, threes, trees, wheeze

2 Syllables

appease, at ease, decrees, deep freeze, degrees, disease, displease, foresees, fresh breeze, light breeze, sea breeze, trapeze

3 Syllables

absentees, blood disease, detainees, devotees, disagrees, expertise, gentle breeze, guarantees, hard to please, heart disease, ill at ease, Japanese, on your knees, overseas, referees, seven seas, skin disease, underseas

Intro
'a'
'e'
'i'
'o'
'u'
'tion'
Word List

Intro

'a'

'e'

'i'

'o'

'u'

'tion'

Word List

4 Syllables

interviewees

5 Syllables

bad luck comes in threes

...ease

(e.g. crease)

see page 88 ...eace (e.g. peace)

...eat

(e.g. heat)

1 Syllable

beat, cheat, eat, feat, feet, fleet, greet, heat, meat,
meet, neat, peat, seat, sheet, sleet, street, suite,
sweet, treat, tweet, wheat

2 Syllables

backseat, back street, charge sheet, compete,
complete, conceit, concrete, crow's feet, dead heat,
deceit, defeat, delete, deplete, discreet, discrete,
downbeat, effete, elite, excrete, high street, hot seat,
Main Street, mistreat, offbeat, petite, raw meat,
receipt, repeat, retreat, white heat

3 Syllables

incomplete, indiscreet, prickly heat, ringside seat,
sausage meat, sugar beet, trick or treat

4 Syllables

beat the retreat, ejection seat, man in the street

...eath

(e.g. wreath)

1 Syllable

heath, sheath, teeth, wreath

2 Syllables

beneath, bequeath

3 Syllables

underneath

...eave

(e.g. leave)

1 Syllable

cleave, eve, grieve, heave, leave, sleeve, we've, weave

2 Syllables

achieve, aggrieve, believe, bereave, conceive, deceive,
naive, perceive, receive, relieve, reprieve, retrieve

3 Syllables

christmas eve, disbelieve, interleave, interweave,
misconceive, new year's eve, one last heave, record
sleeve, time to grieve

4 Syllables

I don't believe, midsummer eve

Intro

'a'

'e'

'i'

'o'

'u'

'tion'

Word List

Intro

'a'

'e'

'i'

'o'

'u'

'tion'

Word List

...ecked
(e.g. wrecked)

1 Syllable
checked, decked, necked, pecked, sect, wrecked

2 Syllables
affect, collect, connect, correct, defect, deflect, deject, detect, direct, dissect, effect, eject, elect, erect, expect, infect, inject, inspect, neglect, object, perfect, project, protect, rechecked, reflect, reject, respect, select, subject, suspect, unchecked

3 Syllables
child neglect, disaffect, disconnect, disinfect, disrespect, incorrect, indirect, interject, intersect, in effect, misdirect, past perfect, recollect, reconnect, redirect, reelect, reinspect, resurrect, side effect, sound effect, take effect

4 Syllables

greenhouse effect, murder suspect, overprotect,
special effect, willful neglect

...ect

(e.g. sect)

see page 102 ...ecked
(e.g. wrecked)

Intro

'a'

'e'

'i'

'o'

'u'

'tion'

Word
List

...ed
(e.g. led)

1 Syllable

bed, bled, bread, bred, dead, dread, fed, head, lead, led, read, red, said, shed, shred, sped, spread, thread, tread, wed

2 Syllables

ahead, brain dead, drop dead, embed, instead, misled, stop dead, unsaid, widespread

3 Syllables

get ahead, infrared, overfed, overhead, seeing red, talking head

4 Syllables

the living dead

...edge

(e.g. ledge)

1 Syllable

dredge, edge, fledge, hedge, ledge, pledge, veg, wedge

...ee

(e.g. see)

1 Syllable

be, bee, fee, flea, flee, free, glee, he, key, knee,

me, plea, quay, sea, see, she, ski, spree, tea, three,

tree, we

2 Syllables

abbey, achy, agree, airy, alley, amply, angry, antsy, any,

army, as he, baby, badly, baggy, balmy, banshee, barely,

105

Intro

'a'

'e'

'i'

'o'

'u'

'tion'

Word
List

barley, beady, beastly, beauty, berry, bitchy, bitsy,

blackly, blandly, blankly, bleakly, bleary, blindly, blithely,

bloody, blowsy, blowy, blowzy, bluntly, blurry, blustery,

body, boggy, boldly, bonny, bony, boogie, booty, boozy,

bossy, bouncy, bounty, brainy, brandy, brashly, brassy,

bravely, brawny, breezy, briefly, brightly, briny, briskly,

broody, bubbly, buddy, bumpy, bunny, burly, bury,

busty, busy, cagey, calmly, candy, canny, carefree, carry,

catchy, catty, cc, C.D., chassis, cheeky, cheery, cheesy,

cherry, chili, chilly, choosy, choppy, city, classy, closely,

cloudy, cockney, cocky, coffee, coldly, comely, comfy,

cookie, copy, corny, country, county, cowry, coyly, cozy,

crazy, cruelly, curvy, daily, daisy, dandy, darkly, deadly,

dearly, deeply, dewy, did he, dimly, dirty, ditty, dizzy,

dreamy, dusky, dusty, duty, early, earthly, empty, ennui,

entry, envy, faintly, fancy, filthy, firmly, firstly, fir tree,

flirty, floozy, foggy, folksy, folly, fondly, foresee, for free,

for me, foxy, frankly, freely, frenzy, frosty, fruit tree,

funky, funny, fury, gaily, genie, gently, ghostly, gipsy,

give me, gladly, glitzy, gloomy, glory, godly, golf tee,

golly, grand prix, greedy, gritty, groupie, guide me,

guilty, gum tree, gusty, gutsy, gypsy, happy, hasty,
hazy, heady, healthy, hearty, heavy, highly, high sea,
high tea, hippie, history, holy, homely, honey, horny,
husky, icy, jetty, jewelry, jolly, journey, junkie, lacy,
lady, laundry, lazy, leggy, lonely, L.P., lucky, madly,
manly, mardy, marquee, marry, maybe, mercy, misery,
misty, money, monkey, moody, mostly, movie, mystery,
nasty, nearly, needy, North Sea, nosey, off-key, oily,
oldie, only, pansy, pantry, parsley, party, peachy,
pebbly, penny, Pepsi, perky, phony, picky, pixie, plenty,
pony, poppy, posy, prairie, pretty, prickly, proudly,
psyche, quirky, rainy, ready, really, ritzy, roadie, rocky,
rosy, roughly, sandy, sassy, saucy, savvy, scot-free,
sentry, set free, settee, sexy, shady, sherry, shyly, silky,
sleepy, smoky, snowy, softly, softy, solely, sorry, starkly,
starry, steady, steamy, steely, stony, stormy, story,
sulky, sultry, sunny, surely, sweetie, sweetly, taxi, teary,
theory, thirsty, thorny, tidy, tightly, tingly, toffee,
trophy, truly, T.V., ugly, warmly, wary, weary, whimsy,
whisky, wildly, windy, witty, worldly, worry, worthy,
yankee, zany, zesty, zingy, zombie

Intro

'a'

'e'

'i'

'o'

'u'

'tion'

Word List

Intro

'a'

'e'

'i'

'o'

'u'

'tion'

Word
List

3 Syllables
absentee, B.B.C., before he, bourgeoisie, busy bee,
christmas tree, come with me, command key, cup of
tea, detainee, disagree, guarantee, how did he,
jubilee, K.G.B., killer bee, M.I.T., M.T.V., master key,
M.P.3., M.P.G., return key, spelling bee, T.N.T.

4 Syllables
admission fee, Aegean sea, afternoon tea, beyond
the sea, family tree, going to be, ignition key, interviewee,
L.A.P.D., master's degree, skeleton key, to some degree

...eed
(e.g. speed)

1 Syllable
bead, bleed, breed, cede, creed, deed, feed, freed,
greed, heed, lead, need, peed, plead, read, reed, seed,
speed, we'd, weed

2 Syllables

agreed, concede, decreed, exceed, force feed, impede, indeed, misdeed, mislead, recede, stampede, succeed, take heed

3 Syllables

chicken feed, disagreed, guaranteed, intercede, overfeed, poppy seed, supersede

...eel

(e.g. feel)

1 Syllable

deal, eel, feel, he'll, heal, heel, keel, kneel, meal, peal, peel, real, reel, seal, she'll, spiel, squeal, steal, steel, we'll, wheel, zeal

Intro

'a'

'e'

'i'

'o'

'u'

'tion'

Word List

2 Syllables

appeal, arms deal, big wheel, conceal, congeal, fair deal, gear wheel, great deal, ideal, ordeal, prayer wheel, raw deal, repeal, reseal, reveal, square deal, surreal, unreal, unseal

3 Syllables

business deal, ferris wheel, potter's wheel, roulette wheel, sex appeal, spinning wheel, stainless steel, steering wheel, wagon wheel, water wheel

4 Syllables

achilles' heel, automobile, banana peel, bicycle wheel, catherine wheel, potato peel, stiletto heel

...eeled
(e.g. peeled)

1 Syllable
field, healed, heeled, reeled, sealed, shield, wheeled,
wield, yield

2 Syllables
appealed, concealed, congealed, force field,
heat shield, mine field, repealed, resealed,
revealed, unsealed

3 Syllables
unconcealed

4 Syllables
magnetic field

...eem

(e.g. seem)

see page 92 ...eam (e.g. dream)

...een

(e.g. seen)

1 Syllable

bean, been, clean, glean, green, kean, keen, lean, mean, preen, Queen, scene, screen, seen, sheen, spleen, teen, wean

2 Syllables

between, caffeine, canteen, convene, demean, foreseen, machine, marine, obscene, onscreen, ravine, routine, serene, smoke screen, steam clean, unclean, unseen, wide screen

3 Syllables

bottle green, golden mean, hallowe'en,
intervene, jelly bean, reconvene, silver screen,
slot machine, submarine, tambourine, tangerine,
tape machine, time machine, trampoline,
unforeseen, wolverine

4 Syllables

computer screen, x-ray machine

...eep
(e.g. weep)

1 Syllable

beep, bleep, cheap, creep, deep, heap, jeep,
keep, leap, peep, reap, seep, sheep, sleep, steep,
sweep, weep

Intro

'a'

'e'

'i'

'o'

'u'

'tion'

Word
List

2 Syllables

asleep, black sheep, dirt cheap, trash heap

3 Syllables

fast asleep, put to sleep, sound asleep

...eered

(e.g. sneered)

see page 95 ...eared
(e.g. feared)

...eet

(e.g. meet)

see page 99 ... eat (e.g. meat)

...eeth

(e.g. teeth)

see page 100 ...eath
(e.g. wreath)

Intro

'a'

'e'

'i'

'o'

'u'

'tion'

Word List

Intro

'a'

'e'

'i'

'o'

'u'

'tion'

Word
List

...eird

(e.g. weird)

see page 95 ...eared (e.g. feared)

...eld

(e.g. held)

1 Syllable

dwelled, felled, held, jelled, meld, quelled, shelled,
smelled, spelled, swelled, weld, yelled

2 Syllables

compelled, dispelled, excelled, expelled, handheld,
impelled, misspelled, propelled, rebelled, repelled,
upheld, withheld

...elf

(e.g. self)

1 Syllable
elf, self, shelf

2 Syllables
herself, himself, itself, myself, yourself

3 Syllables
prove yourself

...ell

(e.g. bell)

1 Syllable
bell, belle, cell, dell, dwell, fell, gel, quell, sell, shell,
smell, spell, swell, tell, well, yell

Intro

'a'

'e'

'i'

'o'

'u'

'tion'

Word List

Intro

'a'

'e'

'i'

'o'

'u'

'tion'

Word List

2 Syllables

as well, blank shell, blood cell, brain cell, cartel, cold spell, compel, death knell, dispel, dry cell, excel, expel, farewell, gaol cell, gazelle, hard sell, hotel, jail cell, like hell, misspell, motel, nerve cell, Noel, oil well, outsell, pastel, propel, rebel, repel, resell, soft sell

3 Syllables

fuel cell, magic spell, personnel, prison cell, say farewell, sense of smell, shotgun shell, solar cell

4 Syllables

detention cell, mademoiselle

...elt

(e.g. felt)

1 Syllable

belt, Celt, dealt, dwelt, felt, knelt, pelt, smelt, svelte, welt

2 Syllables

black belt, fan belt, life belt, seat belt

3 Syllables

bible belt, money belt, safety belt

4 Syllables

asteroid belt, conveyor belt, suspender belt

...em

(e.g. gem)

1 Syllable

femme, gem, stem, them

2 Syllables

brain stem, condemn, F.M., of them, p.m.,

put them

Intro

"a"

"e"

"i"

"o"

"u"

'tion'

Word List

...eme

(e.g. theme)

see page 92 ...eam (e.g. dream)

...en

(e.g. then)

1 Syllable

den, fen, glen, hen, men, pen, ten, then, when, zen

2 Syllables

again, amen, big ben, pig pen, wise men

3 Syllables

ballpoint pen, once again, only when,

then again

4 Syllables

comedienne, gambling den, never again, now and
again, over again, romantic glen, time and again

5 Syllables

again and again, time and time again

7 Syllables

over and over again

...ench
(e.g. bench)

1 Syllable

bench, clench, drench, *mensch*, quench, rench, stench,
tench, trench, wench, wrench

2 Syllables

entrench, retrench

Intro

'a'

'e'

'i'

'o'

'u'

'tion'

Word List

121

3 Syllables

monkey wrench, muscles clench, socket wrench

...end
(e.g. bend)

1 Syllable

bend, blend, fend, friend, lend, mend, penned, send,
spend, tend, trend, wend

2 Syllables

amend, append, ascend, attend, befriend, best
friend, butt end, commend, contend, dead end,
defend, depend, descend, distend, expend, extend,
intend, loose end, offend, pretend, rear end,
suspend, tail end, tightend, transcend, unbend,
West End, year-end

3 Syllables

apprehend, bitter end, comprehend, condescend, in the
end, lady friend, recommend, reoffend, without end

4 Syllables

overextend

...ene

(e.g. scene)

see page 112 ...een (e.g. seen)

...ent

(e.g. sent)

1 Syllable

bent, cent, dent, lent, meant, pent, rent, scent, sent,
spent, tent, vent, went

2 Syllables

accent, ascent, assent, cement, consent, content,
dement, descent, dissent, event, extent, ferment,
intent, invent, lament, misspent, percent, present,
prevent, relent, repent, resent, segment, torment

3 Syllables

circus tent, discontent, malcontent, nonevent,
overspent, pay the rent, reinvent, represent

4 Syllables

happy event, misrepresent

5 Syllables

dramatic event, economic rent, in any event, natural event, recurrent event, to a great extent, underrepresent

...ep
(e.g. step)

1 Syllable

pep, prep, rep, steppe

2 Syllables

misstep, sales rep

Intro
'a'
'e'
'i'
'o'
'u'
'tion'
Word List

...ept
(e.g. kept)

1 Syllable

apt, capped, clapped, crept, flapped, kept,
lapped, leaped, leapt, mapped, napped, prepped,
rapped, rapt, sapped, scrapped, slapped, slept,
snapped, stepped, strapped, swept, tapped, trapped,
wept, wrapped, zapped

2 Syllables

accept, adapt, adept, entrapped, except, inept,
recapped, untapped, unwrapped

3 Syllables

intercept, overslept

...er

(e.g. her)

1 Syllable

birr, blur, cur, er, err, fir, fleur, for, fur, her, myrrh,
purr, sir, slur, spur, stir, were

2 Syllables

bicker, breaker, butter, chaser, chauffeur, cider, clicker,
clutter, cutter, concur, confer, defer, demur, deter,
faker, flicker, flower, flutter, glider, glower, gutter,
incur, infer, inter, kicker, knicker, liqueur, liquor,
mutter, nutter, occur, power, picker, prefer, quicker,
racer, recur, refer, shaker, shower, shutter, sicker,
slicker, slider, snicker, spider, sputter, sticker, strider,
stutter, thicker, ticker, transfer, utter, vicar, wider

3 Syllables

acre, aflutter, baker, bill sticker, collider, connoisseur,
divider, hard liquor, insider, outsider, provider,
reoccur, risk taker, saboteur

Intro

'a'

'e'

'i'

'o'

'u'

'tion'

Word
List

Intro

"a"

"e"

"i"

"o"

"u"

'tion'

Word List

4 Syllables

any hour, circuit breaker, city slicker, cocktail shaker, entrepreneur, legal transfer, wire cutter

…erk
(e.g. jerk)

1 Syllable

berk, clerk, dirk, irk, jerk, kirk, lurk, Merc, murk, perk, quirk, shirk, smirk, Turk, work

2 Syllables

at work, bank clerk, berserk, desk clerk, do work, field work, rework, town clerk, young Turk

3 Syllables

out of work, overwork, social work

4 Syllables
body of work

...erve
(e.g. serve)

1 Syllable
curve, nerve, serve, swerve, verve

2 Syllables
conserve, deserve, observe, preserve, reserve
5 Syllables
federal reserve

Intro

'a'

'e'

'i'

'o'

'u'

'tion'

Word List

Intro

'a'

'e'

'i'

'o'

'u'

'tion'

Word
List

...esh

(e.g. fresh)

1 Syllable
crèche, flesh, fresh, mesh

2 Syllables
afresh, refresh

3 Syllables
in the flesh

...ess

(e.g. bless)

*see also page 134 ...ests
(e.g. nests)*

1 Syllable

bless, dress, guess, guests, less, mess, press, stress,
tress, yes

2 Syllables

address, assess, bequests, caress, compress, confess,
contests, depress, digests, digress, distress, excess,
express, finesse, full dress, impress, infests, invests,
largesse, obsess, oppress, possess, profess, progress,
protests, recess, redress, repress, requests, success,
suggests, suppress, U.S., undress, unless, word stress

3 Syllables

acquiesce, battle dress, coalesce, cocktail dress,
convalesce, dispossess, evening dress, fancy dress,
G.P.S., great success, more or less, reassess, repossess,
wedding dress, what a mess

4 Syllables

civilian dress, nevertheless

'e'

Intro
'a'
'e'
'i'
'o'
'u'
'tion'
Word List

...essed
(e.g. blessed)

see page 132 ...est (e.g. best)

...est
(e.g. best)

1 Syllable

best, blessed, breast, chest, crest, dressed, fessed,
guessed, guest, jest, messed, nest, pest, pressed, rest,
stressed, test, vest, west, wrest, zest

2 Syllables

addressed, arrest, assessed, attest, at rest, bequest,
bird's nest, blood test, compressed, confessed, congest,

contest, depressed, detest, digest, digressed, distressed, divest, expressed, finessed, get dressed, gone West, impressed, infest, ingest, invest, molest, obsessed, oppressed, possessed, professed, progressed, protest, recessed, repressed, request, screen test, suggest, suppressed, tea chest, tool chest, toy chest, transgressed, undressed, unrest, war chest, Wild West

3 Syllables

acid test, acquiesced, chimney breast, coalesced, cuckoo's nest, day of rest, dispossessed, hornet's nest, house arrest, lay to rest, lemon zest, mental test, on request, rearrest, reassessed, reinvest, repossessed, self-professed, treasure chest, unimpressed

4 Syllables

bulletproof vest, medicine chest, ultimate test, unwelcome guest

5 Syllables

cardiac arrest, intelligence test, resisting arrest

Intro

'a'

'e'

'i'

'o'

'u'

'tion'

Word List

...ests
(e.g. nests)
see also page 132 ...ess
(e.g. bless)

1 Syllable
breasts, chests, jests, nests, pests, rests, tests

2 Syllables
arrests, contests, digests, infests, invests, molests,
protests, requests, suggests

...et
(e.g. get)

1 Syllable
bet, debt, fret, get, jet, let, met, net, pet, sweat,
threat, vet, wet, whet, yet

2 Syllables

as yet, bad debt, beset, cadet, cassette, cold sweat, cornet, corvette, drift net, duet, forget, not yet, regret, reset, rosette, roulette, upset, vignette, you bet

3 Syllables

cigarette, coronet, fishing net, in your debt, internet, minaret, not your pet, public debt, silhouette, statuette, suffragette

4 Syllables

mosquito net, national debt, stomach upset

5 Syllables

television set

Intro

'a'

'e'

'i'

'o'

'u'

'tion'

Word
List

...etch
(e.g. fetch)

1 Syllable

etch, fetch, lech, retch, sketch, stretch, wretch

2 Syllables

outstretch

...ew
(e.g. new)

see page 210 ...oo (e.g. too)

...ewd

(e.g. shrewd)

see page 213 ...ood
(e.g. mood)

...ews

(e.g. chews)

see page 221 ...oose
(e.g. choose)

Intro

'a'

'e'

'i'

'o'

'u'

'tion'

Word List

Intro

'a'

'e'

'i'

'o'

'u'

'tion'

Word List

...ice

(e.g. slice)

1 Syllable

dice, ice, lice, mice, nice, price, rice, slice, spice, splice, twice, vice

2 Syllables

advice, concise, cut price, device, entice, precise, think twice

4 Syllables

of men and mice, homing device, storage device, to be precise, warning device, word of advice

5 Syllables

explosive device

6 Syllables

electrical device, electronic device

...ich
(e.g. rich)

1 Syllable

bitch, ditch, glitch, hitch, itch, kitsch, rich, snitch, stitch, switch, twitch, which, witch

2 Syllables

bewitch, enrich, sales pitch

3 Syllables

perfect pitch, wicked witch

4 Syllables

seven year itch

Intro

'a'

'e'

'i'

'o'

'u'

'tion'

Word List

...ick
(e.g. lick)

1 Syllable

blick, brick, chick, click, dick, flick, hick, kick, lick, nick, pick, prick, quick, shtick, sick, slick, stick, thick, tick, trick, wick

2 Syllables

be sick, card trick, cue stick, free kick, ice pick, joss stick, mouse click, nonstick, oil slick, old nick, place kick, pool stick

3 Syllables

control stick, double quick, magic trick, shooting stick, walking stick

4 Syllables

confidence trick, conjuring trick

...icks

(e.g. clicks)

see page 182 ...ix (e.g. fix)

see page 182

...id

(e.g. rid)

1 Syllable

bid, did, grid, hid, kid, lid, mid, quid, rid, skid,

slid, squid

2 Syllables

acid, acrid, acted, aged, amid, arid, baited, beaded,

blighted, blinded, braided, branded, candid, clouded,

coasted, courted, cupid, eyelid, flitted, fluid, forbid,

143

Intro

'a'

'e'

'i'

'o'

'u'

'tion'

Word List

gilded, granted, hated, heeded, horrid, humid, hunted, jaded, jagged, jilted, kindred, languid, liquid, livid, loaded, lucid, lusted, melted, minted, naked, needed, orchid, outbid, outdid, painted, parted, placid, pleaded, ragged, rapid, rigid, sacred, scented, sculpted, shrouded, solid, sordid, sorted, splendid, started, studded, stupid, tainted, tasted, tempted, timid, trusted, twisted, undid, valid, vivid, waited, wanted, wasted, what did, wicked, wilted, winded, wounded, wretched, yielded

3 Syllables

lift the lid, open hearted, power grid

4 Syllables

takeover bid

...ide

(e.g. hide)

1 Syllable

bide, bride, chide, cried, died, dried, dyed, eyed,
fried, glide, guide, hide, lied, pied, pride, pried, ride,
shied, side, sighed, slide, snide, spied, stride, tide,
tied, tried, wide

2 Syllables

abide, allied, applied, aside, astride, beside, bright
side, collide, complied, confide, decide, defied, denied,
deride, divide, far side, feel pride, hair slide, hang
glide, high tide, implied, inside, low tide, misguide,
outside, pool-side, preside, provide, relied, replied,
reside, slack tide, stateside, subside, supplied, take
pride, tongue tied, untied, untried, upside, West Side,
with pride, worldwide

Intro

'a'

'e'

'i'

'o'

'u'

'tion'

Word List

3 Syllables

alongside, bring outside, brush aside, cast aside, civic
pride, coincide, far and wide, great divide, lay aside,
nationwide, on the side, push aside, rising tide, set
aside, side by side, upper side, woe betide

4 Syllables

Jekyll and Hyde, on the far side

...ie

(e.g. lie)

1 Syllable

aye, buy, by, bye, cry, die, dry, dye, eye, fly, fry, guy, hi,
high, I, lie, my, nigh, pi, pie, ply, pry, rye, shy, sigh, sky,
sly, spry, spy, thigh, tie, try, vie, why, wry

2 Syllables

ally, and I, apply, awry, bad guy, Bandai, bird's eye,
black eye, black tie, blow fly, blue sky, bone dry,
bonsai, bow tie, bull's eye, but I, bye-bye, cat's eye,
come by, comply, crossed eye, cup tie, decry, defy,
deny, drop by, fall guy, fly by, fly high, fruit fly, get by,
glass eye, goodbye, good guy, go by, hair dye, hi-fi,
horse fly, if I, imply, in my, July, let fly, live by, meat
pie, mince pie, mind's eye, nearby, pass by, pork pie,
rabbi, rely, reply, retry, run by, run dry, scrape by,
Shanghai, sit by, slide by, slip by, small fry, squeak by,
squeeze by, standby, stand by, stick by, stir fry, supply,
thereby, tough guy, untie, wise guy

3 Syllables

abide by, apple pie, by and by, by the bye,
evil eye, exist by, hook and eye, in reply,
old school tie, on the sly, private eye, public eye,
travel by, underlie

4 Syllables
blink of an eye, fourth of July, give it a try, give the glad
eye, money supply, see eye to eye, turn a blind eye

5 Syllables
dominated by, steak and kidney pie

...ie

(e.g. boogie)

see page 105 ...ee (e.g. see)

...ied

(e.g. cried)

see page 145 ...ide (e.g. hide)

...ies
(e.g. tries)

see page 174 ...ise (e.g. rise)

...ife
(e.g. life)

1 Syllable

knife, life, rife, strife, wife

2 Syllables

bread knife, fish wife

3 Syllables

carving knife, hunting knife, kitchen knife, man and wife, pocket knife

4 Syllables

surgical knife, trouble and strife

...ift
(e.g. lift)

1 Syllable

drift, gift, lift, miffed, rift, shift, shrift, sift, sniffed, stiffed, swift, thrift

2 Syllables

adrift, day shift, fork-lift, night shift, short shrift, work shift

3 Syllables

graveyard shift, wedding gift

...ig

(e.g. dig)

1 Syllable

big, brig, fig, gig, jig, pig, prig, rig, swig, twig,
Whig, wig

2 Syllables

drill rig, mine pig, oil rig

3 Syllables

drilling rig, guinea pig, offshore rig,
suckling pig

...ight

(e.g. light)

see page 179 ...ite (e.g. spite)

...ike

(e.g. like)

1 Syllable

bike, dyke, hike, like, mike, pike, spike, strike

2 Syllables

alike, dislike, tax hike, unlike

3 Syllables

hunger strike, on your bike, mountain bike

...ild

(e.g. wild)

1 Syllable

child, filed, mild, piled, riled, smiled, styled, tiled,
wild, wiled

2 Syllables

beguiled, compiled, love child, refiled, restyled,
reviled, with child

3 Syllables

in the wild, missing child

...ile
(e.g. pile)

1 Syllable
pile, guile, rile, stile, style, tile, vile, while, wile

2 Syllables
agile, beguile, fertile, fragile, hair style, hostile, life style, new style, old style, restyle, revile, trash pile, trial, worthwhile

3 Syllables
all the while, emerald isle, for a while, rank and file, single file, versatile

...ill

(e.g. hill)

1 Syllable

bill, chill, dill, drill, fill, frill, gill, grill, grille, hill, ill, kill, mill, nil, pill, shrill, sill, skill, spill, still, swill, thrill, till, we'll, will

2 Syllables

distil(l), downhill, free will, fulfil(l), goodwill, ill will, instil(l), stand still, until, uphill

3 Syllables

dollar bill, dressed to kill, overspill, poison pill, power drill

4 Syllables

electric drill, medical bill, mentally ill, suicide pill, telephone bill

5 Syllables

hundred dollar bill, superior skill

Intro

'a'

'e'

'i'

'o'

'u'

'tion'

Word List

...ilt

(e.g. tilt)

1 Syllable

built, gilt, guilt, hilt, jilt, kilt, lilt, quilt, silt, spilt, tilt, wilt

2 Syllables

rebuilt, unbuilt

3 Syllables

to the hilt

...im
(e.g. skim)

1 Syllable

brim, dim, grim, gym, him, hymn, limb, prim, rim,
sim, skim, slim, swim, trim, vim, whim

2 Syllables

hind limb

3 Syllables

on a whim, phantom limb

...ime
(e.g. time)

1 Syllable

chime, climb, crime, dime, grime, i'm, lime, mime,
prime, rhyme, slime, thyme, time

2 Syllables

one-time, part-time, sublime, war crime, wild thyme

3 Syllables

rapid climb, the sublime

4 Syllables

internal rhyme, nursery rhyme, organized crime,
partner in crime, victimless crime

...in

(e.g. win)

1 Syllable

been, bin, chin, din, fin, gin, grin, inn, kin, pin, shin, sin, skin, spin, tin, twin, when, win

2 Syllables

begin, has been, have been, sequin, sloe gin, tail fin, thick skin, trash bin, within

3 Syllables

deadly sin, drawing pin, mickey finn, mortal sin, next of kin, rolling pin, safety pin, violin

4 Syllables

animal skin, siamese twin

5 Syllables

identical twin, original sin, take it on the chin

...ind
(e.g. mind)

Intro

'a'

'e'

'i'

'o'

'u'

'tion'

Word
List

1 Syllable

bind, blind, dined, find, fined, grind, hind, kind, lined,
mind, mined, rind, shined, signed, wind, wined

2 Syllables

aligned, assigned, behind, confined, consigned,
declined, defined, designed, enshrined, entwined,
inclined, maligned, mankind, refined, remind,
resigned, unkind, unsigned, unwind

3 Syllables

bear in mind, change your mind, come to mind,
disinclined, drop behind, fall behind, frame of
mind, get behind, have in mind, intertwined, in
the mind, leave behind, of one mind, of sound
mind, open mind, peace of mind, realigned,

reassigned, redefined, redesigned, slip your mind,
spring to mind, state of mind, unconfined,
undefined, undermined, unrefined

4 Syllables

in your right mind, make up your mind, of the same
mind, of unsound mind, presence of mind,
subconscious mind, time out of mind,
unconscious mind

...ind

(e.g. rescind)

see page 166 ...inned
(e.g. sinned)

...ine
(e.g. fine)

1 Syllable

brine, dine, fine, line, mine, nine, pine, shine, shrine, sign, spine, swine, twine, vine, whine, wine

2 Syllables

align, assign, benign, blood line, branch line, bread line, chalk line, cloud nine, combine, confine, consign, decline, define, design, divine, enshrine, entwine, goal line, incline, land mine, life line, malign, phone line, plot line, punch line, plus sign, red wine, refine, resign, straight line, street sign, v sign

3 Syllables

by design, disincline, dollar sign, equals sign, fall in line, finish line, firing line, hold the line, intertwine, minus sign, party line, picket line, power line,

realign, reassign, recombine, redefine, redesign,
starting line, toe the line, waiting line, water line,
wine and dine

4 Syllables

assembly line, poverty line, telephone line,
top of the line

6 Syllables

interior design, unemployment line

...ined
(e.g. lined)

see page 160 ...ind (e.g. mind)

163

...ing

(e.g. sing)

1 Syllable

bling, bring, Ching, cling, ding, fling, king, ping, ring, schwing, sing, sling, spring, sting, string, swing, thing, wing, wring, zing

2 Syllables

bee sting, Beijing, biding, chiding, gas ring, gin sling, gliding, guiding, hot spring, key ring, left wing, prize ring, purse string, real thing, riding, right wing, shoe string, striding, sun king, upswing, whole thing

3 Syllables

apron string, baseball swing, boxing ring, fairy ring, Highland fling, in full swing, living thing, on the wing, providing, subsiding, wedding ring

4 Syllables

engagement ring, rotary wing

3 Syllables

abiding, colliding, confiding, deciding, deriding,

dividing, residing, subsiding

...ink

(e.g. think)

1 Syllable

blink, brink, chink, clink, dink, drink, inc., ink, link,

mink, pink, plink, rink, shrink, sink, stink, sync, think,

wink, zinc

2 Syllables

hard drink, ice rink, lip sync, rethink

Intro

'a'

'e'

'i'

'o'

'u'

'tion'

Word
List

3 Syllables

kitchen sink, missing link, skating rink

5 Syllables

indelible ink

...inned
(e.g. sinned)

1 Syllable

binned, chinned, dinned, grinned, pinned,
shinned, sinned, skinned, tinned,
twinned, wind

2 Syllables

downwind, rescind, sequinned, tailwind,
upwind, woodwind

Intro

3 Syllables

underpinned

...int

(e.g. mint)

'a'

'e'

'i'

1 Syllable

dint, flint, glint, hint, lint, mint, print, splint, sprint,
squint, stint, tint

'o'

2 Syllables

didn't, imprint, long stint, misprint, reprint

'u'

3 Syllables

out of print

'tion'

Word List

...ip
(e.g. slip)

1 Syllable

chip, clip, dip, drip, flip, grip, hip, lip, nip, pip, quip, rip, ship, sip, skip, slip, snip, strip, tip, trip, whip, zip

2 Syllables

equip, film clip, unzip

3 Syllables

cartoon strip, comic strip, ego trip, landing strip, microchip, pirate ship, skinny dip

4 Syllables

bargaining chip, silicon chip

...ipe
(e.g. wipe)

1 Syllable

gripe, hype, pipe, ripe; snipe, stripe, swipe, type, wipe

2 Syllables

blood type, soil pipe, waste pipe

3 Syllables

body type, exhaust pipe, overripe, water pipe

...ir
(e.g. stir)

see page 127 ...er (e.g. her)

...ird
(e.g. bird)

1 Syllable

bird, blurred, curd, heard, herd, nerd, slurred, spurred, stirred, word

2 Syllables

absurd, chauffeured, deferred, demurred, deterred, key word, misheard, preferred, recurred, referred, unheard

3 Syllables

overheard, spoken word, undeterred, weasel word, word for word

...ire

(e.g. fire)

1 Syllable

dire, fire, hire, ire, mire, sire, spire, tire, tyre, wire

2 Syllables

admire, afire, acquire, aspire, barbed wire, briar, buyer, ceasefire, choir, conspire, crier, cross wire, desire, drier, dryer, dyer, enquire, entire, expire, flier, flyer, fryer, high wire, higher, inquire, inspire, liar, live wire, misfire, perspire, plier, prior, require, rewire, saphire, transpire, trier, trip wire

3 Syllables

ball of fire, forest fire, line of fire, open fire, set on fire, under fire

Intro

'a'

'e'

'i'

'o'

'u'

'tion'

Word
List

4 Syllables
piano wire, telephone wire

5 Syllables
sexual desire

...irm
(e.g. firm)

1 Syllable
firm, germ, sperm, squirm, sturm, term, worm

2 Syllables
affirm, confirm, full term, infirm

3 Syllables
prison term, reaffirm, reconfirm

...irred

(e.g. stirred)

see page 170 ...ird (e.g. bird)

...irt

(e.g. dirt)

see page 276 ...urt (e.g. hurt)

Intro

'a'

'e'

'i'

'o'

'u'

'tion'

Word List

...ise
(e.g. rise)

1 Syllable

buys, cries, dies, dyes, eyes, flies, fries, guys, guise,
highs, lies, pies, prize, rise, shies, sighs, size, skies,
spies, thighs, ties, tries, wise

2 Syllables

advise, allies, applies, arise, baptize, chastise,
comprise, defies, demise, denies, despise, devise,
disguise, excise, french fries, give rise, goodbyes,
implies, incise, pint-size, relies, replies, snake eyes,
supplies, surprise, unwise, upsize

3 Syllables

improvise, nobel prize, organize, oversize, underlies

5 Syllables

decriminalize, sensationalize

74

...isp
(e.g. crisp)

1 Syllable
crisp, lisp, wisp

...iss
(e.g. miss)

1 Syllable
bliss, dis, hiss, kiss, liss, lists, miss, this

2 Syllables
abyss, amiss, assists, at this, dismiss, does this, french kiss, furnace, in this

3 Syllables
reminisce

Intro

'a'

'e'

'i'

'o'

'u'

'tion'

Word List

...issed

(e.g. missed)

see below ...ist (e.g. mist)

...ist

(e.g. mist)

1 Syllable

fist, gist, hissed, kissed, list, midst, missed, mist,
pissed, twist, wist, wrist

2 Syllables

assist, clenched fist, desist, dismissed, enlist, exist,
insist, persist, price list, resist, short list, sick list,
stock list, subsist

3 Syllables

coexist, mailing list, reminisced, waiting list

...it
(e.g. sit)

1 Syllable

bit, Brit, chit, fit, flit, grit, hit, it, kit, knit, lit, nit, pit, quit, sit, skit, slit, spit, split, whit, wit, writ, zit

2 Syllables

acquit, admit, commit, cool it, do it, get it, hoof it, leg it, lose it, make it, omit, on it, permit, snuff it, submit, tool kit, transmit, unfit

3 Syllables

about it, ask for it, bit by bit, holy writ, isn't it, loosely knit, see to it, size of it, take a hit, throw a fit, work permit, you said it

4 Syllables
every bit

5 Syllables
have a go at it, on the face of it

...itch
(e.g. stitch)

see page 141 ...ich (e.g. rich)

...ite
(e.g. spite)

1 Syllable

bite, blight, bright, fight, flight, fright, height, kite, knight, light, lite, might, mite, night, plight, quite, right, rite, sight, site, slight, spite, sprite, tight, trite, white, write

2 Syllables

alight, alright, arc light, bomb site, brake light, contrite, delight, despite, dog bite, excite, first light, forthright, gang fight, good night, green light, hold tight, ignite, incite, indict, invite, in flight, in sight, itch mite, just right, knife fight, land site, onsite, outright, polite, rear light, recite, red light, rewrite, sit tight, sound bite, stage fright, stage right, take flight, this night, tonight, twelfth night, upright, uptight, white knight, with spite

Intro

'a'

'e'

'i'

'o'

'u'

'tion'

Word List

Intro

'a'

'e'

'i'

'o'

'u'

'tion'

Word
List

3 Syllables

at first sight, beam of light, black and white,
building site, camping site, civil right, come to light,
guiding light, human right, inner light, insect bite,
leading light, legal right, line of sight, nonstop flight,
out of sight, overnight, overwrite, pilot light,
ray of light, reignite, reinvite, reunite, second sight,
shaft of light, speed of light, traffic light,
warning light, water right, water sprite,
wedding night

4 Syllables

burial site, city of light, domestic flight, electric light,
every night, exclusive right, infrared light,
midsummer night, mosquito bite, opening
night, overexcite, Queen of the night,
sweetness and light

...ive

(e.g. give)

1 Syllable
give, live, sieve

2 Syllables
forgive, outlive, relive

3 Syllables
work to live

...ive

(e.g. dive)

1 Syllable
dive, drive, five, hive, jive, live, strive, thrive

Intro

'a'

'e'

'i'

'o'

'u'

'tion'

Word List

2 Syllables

alive, arrive, contrive, deprive, revive, sex drive,
survive

3 Syllables

come alive

5 Syllables

protect and survive

...ix
(e.g. fix)

1 Syllable

bricks, chicks, clicks, dicks, flicks, hicks, kicks, Knicks,
licks, mix, nicks, nix, picks, pics, pix, pricks, ricks,
slicks, sticks, ticks, tics, tricks, Vicks, wicks

2 Syllables

conflicts, depicts, inflicts, predicts, transfix

3 Syllables

bag of tricks, row of bricks

...ize

(e.g. prize)

see page 174 ...ise (e.g. risc)

Intro

'a'

'e'

'i'

'o'

'u'

'tion'

Word List

Intro

'a'

'e'

'i'

'o'

'u'

'tion'

Word List

...o

(e.g. go)

1 Syllable

beau, blow, bow, bro', co., crow, doe, doh, dough,
flow, foe, fro', go, grow, know, low, mow, no, oh, owe,
pro, row, sew, show, slow, snow, so, sow, though,
throw, toe, tow, whoa, woe

2 Syllables

ago, although, and co., and so, below, dumb show, floor
show, game show, golf pro, hello, John Doe, laid low, let
go, lie low, make grow, nouveau, or so, outgrow, plateau,
road show, so-so, strip show, talk show, tarot, you know

3 Syllables

C.E.O., even so, ever so, golden glow, let it go, long
ago, overflow, picture show, puppet show, quid pro
quo, shadow show, status quo, tallyho, tidal flow,
time to go, to and fro, T.V. show, U.F.O., undergo

4 Syllables

carrion crow, from head to toe

5 Syllables

television show, a long time ago

...oach

(e.g. coach)

1 Syllable

broach, brooch, coach, poach, roach

2 Syllables

approach, encroach, reproach

....oad

(e.g. road)

see page 197 ...ode (e.g. rode)

...oak

(e.g. soak)

1 Syllable

bloke, broke, choke, cloak, coke, croak, folk, joke, oak,
poke, smoke, soak, spoke, stoke, stroke, woke, yoke, yolk

2 Syllables

awoke, evoke, ground stroke, gun smoke, invoke,
misspoke, provoke, revoke, sick joke

3 Syllables
dirty joke, killing joke

4 Syllables
practical joke

5 Syllables
automatic choke

...oam
(c.g. roam)

1 Syllable
chrome, comb, dome, foam, home, roam

2 Syllables
go home, rest home, shalom

Intro

'a'

'e'

'i'

'o'

'u'

'tion'

Word List

Intro

'a'

'e'

'i'

'o'

'u'

'tion'

Word
List

3 Syllables

foster home, motor home, nursing home

4 Syllables

funeral home

...oar

(e.g. soar)

see page 80 ...aw (e.g. saw)

...oast

(e.g. boast)

1 Syllable

boast, coast, ghost, grossed, host, most, post, roast,

toast

2 Syllables

at most, engrossed, french toast, Gold Coast

3 Syllables

at the most, command post, diagnosed, holy ghost,

trading post, winning post

4 Syllables

deaf as a post, telegraph post

5 Syllables

from pillar to post, military post, missionary post,

observation post

Intro

'a'

'e'

'i'

'o'

'u'

'tion'

Word List

...oat
(e.g. throat)

1 Syllable

bloat, boat, coat, dote, float, gloat, goat, moat, mote, note, oat, quote, rote, throat, tote, vote, wrote

2 Syllables

afloat, bank note, demote, denote, devote, misquote, promote, remote, rewrote, uncoat, unquote, whole note

3 Syllables

right to vote

Intro

'a'

'e'

'i'

'o'

'u'

'tion'

Word List

...ob

(e.g. sob)

1 Syllable

blob, bob, cob, glob, gob, hob, job, knob, lob, mob, rob, slob, snob, sob, swab, throb

2 Syllables

hand job, lynch mob, nose job

3 Syllables

hatchet job, inside job, on the job

Intro

'a'

'e'

'i'

'o'

'u'

'tion'

Word List

Intro

'a'

'e'

'i'

'o'

'u'

'tion'

Word
List

...obe
(e.g. probe)

1 Syllable
globe, lobe, robe, strobe

3 Syllables
frontal lobe

...ock
(e.g. lock)

1 Syllable
block, chock, clock, cock, crock, dock, flock, knock, lock,
mock, rock, shock, sock, stock, talk, tock, walk

2 Syllables

dreadlock, o'clock, take stock, unlock

3 Syllables

alarm clock, building block, chopping block, city block, interlock, mental block, office block, rolling stock, round the clock, starting block, tower block, writer's block

4 Syllables

against the clock, around the clock, stumbling block

5 Syllables

electrical shock

...ocks
(e.g. rocks)

see page 251 ...ox (e.g. box)

...odd
(e.g. odd)

1 Syllable

god, nod, odd, plod, pod, rod, shod, sod, squad,
trod, wad

2 Syllables

hot rod, roughshod, vice squad, tight-wad, war god

Intro

'a'

'e'

'i'

'o'

'u'

'tion'

Word
List

3 Syllables

act of God, firing squad, flying squad, house of God, lightning rod, ride roughshod, word of God

4 Syllables

city of God, kingdom of God, measuring rod, olympic God

...ode
(e.g. rode)

1 Syllable

blowed, bode, bowed, code, crowed, flowed, glowed, goad, load, mode, mowed, node, ode, owed, road, rode, owed, sewed, showed, slowed, snowed, sowed, stowed, strode, toad, towed

Intro
'a'
'e'
'i'
'o'
'u'
'tion'
Word List

Intro

'a'

'e'

'i'

'o'

'u'

'tion'

Word List

2 Syllables

abode, busload, case load, commode, corrode, decode, encode, erode, explode, forebode, implode, main road, morse code, plateaued, reload, ring road, side road, source code, tailed toad, trunk road, unbowed, unload, zip code

3 Syllables

à la mode, on the road, overflowed, penal code, private road, secret code

4 Syllables

computer code, ethical code

...off

(e.g. off)

1 Syllable

cough, doff, off, prof., scoff, trough

...oil

(e.g. coil)

1 Syllable

oil, boil, broil, coil, foil, roil, soil, spoil, toil

2 Syllables

gold foil, recoil, tin foil, uncoil

Intro

'a'

'e'

'i'

'o'

'u'

'tion'

Word List

...oint
(e.g. disappoint)

1 Syllable
joint, point

2 Syllables
anoint, appoint, disjoint, flash point, knee joint,

weak point

3 Syllables
boiling point, breaking point, disappoint, elbow joint,

focal point, freezing point, make a point, melting

point, reappoint, to the point, turning point

4 Syllables
vanishing point

5 Syllables
artificial joint

...oke

(e.g. poke)

see page 188 ...oak (e.g. soak)

...old

(e.g. cold)

1 Syllable

bold, bowled, cold, doled, fold, gold, hold, holed, mold, mould, old, polled, rolled, scold, sold, strolled, told, tolled

2 Syllables

all told, behold, cajoled, consoled, controlled, enfold, enrolled, extolled, fool's gold, get hold, outsold, paroled, patrolled, take hold, unfold, unsold, untold, uphold, white gold, withhold

3 Syllables

oversold, taking hold, uncontrolled, undersold

...ole

(e.g. hole)

1 Syllable

bole, bowl, coal, dole, droll, foal, goal, knoll, mole, ol',
ole, pole, poll, role, roll, scroll, sole, soul, stole, stroll,
toll, troll, whole

2 Syllables

cajole, console, control, dead soul, dust bowl, enroll,
extol, parole, patrol, punch bowl, soup bowl, south
pole, spring roll

3 Syllables

arms control, as a whole, birth control, crowd control, gun control, heart and soul, lose control, on the whole, price control, rock'n'roll, sausage roll, self-control, take control, title role, toilet bowl, toilet roll, totem pole

4 Syllables

beyond control, body and soul, magnetic pole, remote control, telegraph pole, under control

...olk

(e.g. folk)

see page 188 ...oak (e.g. soak)

Intro

'a'

'e'

'i'

'o'

'u'

'tion'

Word List

...oll
(e.g. roll)

see page 202 ...ole (e.g. hole)

...olt
(e.g. colt)

1 Syllable
bolt, colt, jolt, volt

2 Syllables
revolt

3 Syllables
nut and bolt, safety bolt

...olve

(e.g. solve)

1 Syllable

solve

2 Syllables

absolve, devolve, dissolve, evolve, involve, resolve, revolve

...om

(e.g. prom)

1 Syllable

alm, balm, bomb, from, glom, homme, mom, palm,
pom, prom

2 Syllables

aplomb, embalm, flow from, keep from, shalom,
shrink from, wring from

Intro

'a'

'e'

'i'

'u'

'tion'

Word List

'o'

...ome

(e.g. home)

see page 189 ...oam (e.g. roam)

...ome

(e.g. come)

1 Syllable

bum, chum, crumb, drum, dumb, from, glum, gum,
mum, numb, plum, plumb, rum, scum, slum, some,
strum, sum, thumb

2 Syllables

become, flow from, keep from, keep mum, shrink
from, succumb, wring from

3 Syllables

bubble gum, chewing gum, drunken bum, rule of thumb, spirit gum

...on
(e.g. on)

1 Syllable

brawn, con, dawn, drawn, fawn, gone, hon., lawn, pawn, scone, shone, spawn, swan, wan, won, yawn

2 Syllables

baton, c'mon, come-on, for(e)gone, outshone, run-on, salon, upon, withdrawn

3 Syllables

feed upon, frown upon, goings-on, look upon, overdrawn, undergone

Intro

'a'

'e'

'i'

'o'

'u'

'tion'

Word List

4 Syllables

agreed upon, beauty salon, depend upon

...one

(e.g. stone)

1 Syllable

blown, bone, clone, cone, crone, don', flown, groan, grown, hone, known, loan, lone, moan, own, phone, prone, scone, sewn, shown, sown, stone, throne, thrown, tone, zone

2 Syllables

alone, atone, bemoan, cologne, condone, cyclone, disown, drop zone, homegrown, intone, outgrown, postpone, unknown, well known

3 Syllables

combat zone, danger zone, fully grown, let alone,
muscle tone, on their own, on your own, overblown,
overgrown, overthrown

...ong
(e.g. long)

1 Syllable

gong, long, pong, song, strong, thong, throng, wrong

2 Syllables

along, belong, folk song, go wrong, lifelong, prolong,
sarong, swan song, torch song

3 Syllables

all along, come along, for a song, get along, play
along, rub along, string along, tag along

Intro

'a'

'e'

'i'

'o'

'u'

'tion'

Word List

5 Syllables
sense of right and wrong

....OO
(e.g. too)

1 Syllable
blew, blue, brew, chew, clue, coup, crew, cue,
dew, do, drew, few, flew, flu, flue, glue, grew,
loo, ooh, phew, queue, rue, screw, shoe, shoo,
sioux, skew, slew, spew, stew, sue, threw, through,
thru, to, too, true, two, view, *vue*, whew, who,
woo, you, zoo

2 Syllables
accrue, add to, adieu, ado, all too, and to,
and you, anew, askew, as to, a few, bamboo,

belle vue, break through, breeze through, canoe, cling to, close to, come through, come to, construe, cut through, cut to, deaf to, debut, did you, do you, due to, ensue, eschew, fall through, get through, get to, got to, got you, go through, go to, ground crew, gym shoe, have to, have you, home brew, how to, if you, imbue, into, in view, kung fu, look to, make do, new to, not due, ooze through, ought to, outdo, outgrew, out to, pass through, pool cue, pull through, pursue, push through, put through, ragu, redo, renew, review, run through, sail through, see through, shampoo, side view, soak through, speak to, squeak through, stage crew, stick to, stoop to, subdue, sweep through, taboo, take to, tattoo, tell you, thank you, that you, time to, to do, to you, true blue, true to, turn to, undo, unglue, untrue, up to, used to, want to, warm to, whip through, wise to, withdrew, work through, world view, would you, you do, you to, you too

Intro

'a'

'e'

'i'

'o'

'u'

'tion'

Word List

3 Syllables

bomber crew, book review, break into, bump into, buy into, conform to, crazy glue, cut into, déja vu, equal to, extend to, fall into, field of view, follow through, get into, going to, good for you, grow into, in full view, irish stew, kangaroo, lay into, lay waste to, live up to, look into, look up to, misconstrue, out of view, overdo, overdue, overthrew, peacock blue, point of view, powder blue, resort to, respect to, royal blue, running shoe, run into, slice into, stomach flu, subject to, subscribe to, supposed to, talking to, talk into, tear into, through and through, Timbuktu, travel to, turn into, what are you, what did you, what do you, you have to, you want to

4 Syllables

angle of view, hullabaloo, long-overdue, out of the blue

...ood
(e.g. mood)

1 Syllable

booed, brewed, brood, chewed, clued, crude, cued,
dude, feud, food, glued, hued, lewd, mood, nude,
prude, rude, screwed, shrewd, skewed, spewed,
stewed, sued, viewed, who'd, wooed, you'd

2 Syllables

allude, blood feud, canned food, collude, conclude,
construed, debuted, delude, elude, ensued,
exclude, exude, imbued, include, intrude, pursued,
renewed, reviewed, seclude, shampooed,
subdued, tattooed, unglued

3 Syllables

frozen food, misconstrued, takeout food

Intro
'a'
'e'
'i'
'u'
'tion'
Word List

...ood

(e.g. wood)

1 Syllable

could, good, hood, should, stood, wood, would, you'd

2 Syllables

do good, for good, make good, withstood

3 Syllables

common good, Robin Hood, understood

4 Syllables

misunderstood

...oof

(e.g. roof)

1 Syllable
goof, hoof, roof, pouf

2 Syllables
aloof

...ook

(e.g. look)

see also page 261 ...uke
(e.g. fluke)

1 Syllable
book, brook, cook, crook, hook, look, nook,

rook, shook, took

2 Syllables

boat hook, closed book, phone book, prayer book,
unbook, unhook

3 Syllables

grappling hook, overcook, overtook, undercook,
undertook

4 Syllables

telephone book

5 Syllables

by hook or by crook

Intro

'a'

'e'

'i'

'o'

'u'

'tion'

Word List

...ool

(e.g. cool)

1 Syllable

cool, drool, fool, pool, rule, school, spool, stool, tool, who'll, you'll

2 Syllables

cruel, dual, duel, fuel, jewel, uncool, you fool

3 Syllables

golden rule, I'm no fool, supercool

...ool

(e.g. wool)

see page 262 ...ull (e.g. pull)

...oom

(e.g. room)

1 Syllable

bloom, boom, broom, doom, fume, gloom,
groom, loom, plume, room, tomb, vroom, whom,
womb, zoom

2 Syllables

assume, ballroom, consume, costume, entomb,
exhume, headroom, kaboom, legroom, mushroom,
perfume, presume, resume, vacuum, volume

3 Syllables

baby boom, nom de plume, reassume, sonic boom

4 Syllables

swimming costume

Intro

'a'

'e'

'i'

'o'

'u'

'tion'

Word
List

...oon

(e.g. moon)

1 Syllable

boon, croon, dune, goon, hewn, loon, moon, noon,
prune, soon, spoon, strewn, swoon, toon, tune

2 Syllables

attune, baboon, balloon, buffoon, cartoon, cocoon,
commune, harpoon, high noon, immune, impugn,
lagoon, monsoon, saloon, sand dune, soup spoon,
too soon, twelve noon, tycoon, typhoon

3 Syllables

afternoon, opportune, silver spoon

4 Syllables

good afternoon, inopportune, signature tune

...ooned
(e.g. swooned)

1 Syllable

crooned, mooned, pruned, spooned, swooned,
tuned, wound

2 Syllables

attuned, ballooned, cartooned, communed,
dragooned, festooned, harpooned, marooned,
unpruned, raw wound, war wound

... oor
(e.g. poor)

see page 80 ...aw (e.g. saw)

...oose

(e.g. choose)

see page 233 ...ose (e.g. lose)

...oose

(e.g. goose)

1 Syllable

abuse, deuce, goose, juice, loose, moose, mousse,
noose, puce, spruce, truce, use, Zeus

2 Syllables

deduce, diffuse, disuse, excuse, footloose, induce,
misuse, mongoose, obtuse, produce, profuse, recluse,
reduce, refuse, seduce, vamoose

...oot

(e.g. root)

Intro

'a'

'e'

'i'

'o'

'u'

'tion'

Word List

1 Syllable

boot, brute, cute, flute, foot, fruit, hoot, loot, lute, moot,
mute, newt, put, root, route, scoot, shoot, suit, toot

2 Syllables

acute, astute, Beirut, bus route, coal chute, commute,
compute, dilute, dispute, dried fruit, en route, grassroot,
ill repute, impute, jump suit, minute, pollute, pursuit,
recruit, refute, repute, reroute, salute, sweat suit, uproot

3 Syllables

absolute, bamboo shoot, birthday suit, boiler suit,
business suit, cowboy boot, disrepute, follow suit,
give a hoot, in dispute, passion fruit, pressure suit,
raw recruit, stay put

4 Syllables

forbidden fruit, underfoot

...ooth
(e.g. smooth)

1 Syllable
smooth, soothe

...ooth
(e.g. tooth)

1 Syllable
booth, sleuth, sooth, tooth, truth, youth

2 Syllables
dogtooth, eyetooth, tollbooth, uncouth,
untruth, vermouth

...ooze

(e.g. ooze)

see page 233 ...ose (e.g. lose)

...op

(e.g. top)

1 Syllable

bop, chop, cop, crop, drop, flop, hop, lop, mop, op,

plop, pop, prop, shop, slop, sop, stop, swap, top

2 Syllables

big top, bus stop, full stop, nonstop, speed cop,

talk shop

Intro

'a'

'e'

'i'

'o'

'u'

'tion'

Word List

3 Syllables

hunting crop, soda pop, spinning top, traffic cop,

whistle stop

5 Syllables

motorcycle cop

...ope

(e.g. rope)

1 Syllable

cope, dope, grope, hope, lope, mope, nope, pope,

rope, scope, slope, soap

2 Syllables

bath soap, elope, face soap, tightrope

3 Syllables

forlorn hope

4 Syllables

Cape of Good Hope

5 Syllables

continental slope

...or
(e.g. for)

see page 80 ...aw (e.g. saw)

...orch

(e.g. torch)

1 Syllable

porch, scorch, torch

...ork

(e.g. fork)

see page 42 ...alk (e.g. walk)

...orm
(e.g. form)

1 Syllable

dorm, form, norm, storm, swarm, warm

2 Syllables

age norm, conform, deform, dust storm, ice storm,
inform, lukewarm, perform, reform, transform

3 Syllables

misinform

4 Syllables

electric storm, magnetic storm, meteor swarm,
violent storm

5 Syllables

electrical storm

7 Syllables

operation desert storm

...orn

(e.g. worn)

1 Syllable

born, brawn, corn, dawn, drawn, fawn, horn, lawn,
mourn, pawn, porn, scorn, shorn, spawn, sworn,
thorn, torn, warn, yawn

2 Syllables

adorn, car horn, firstborn, forlorn, reborn, stillborn,
unborn, withdrawn

3 Syllables

overdrawn, unadorn

Intro

'a'

'e'

'i'

'o'

'u'

'tion'

Word List

Intro

"a"

"e"

"i"

"o"

"u"

'tion'

Word
List

...orce
(e.g. force)

1 Syllable

coarse, course, force, hoarse, horse, sauce, source

2 Syllables

clotheshorse, concourse, discourse, divorce, endorse,
enforce, packhorse, racecourse, racehorse, recourse,
remorse, resource, seahorse, warhorse, workhorse

...ort
(e.g. sport)

see also page 137 ...ot (e.g. hot)

1 Syllable

bought, brought, caught, court, fort, fought, fraught,
naught, ought, port, short, sort, sought, sport, taught,
taut, thought, wart, wrought

2 Syllables

abort, airport, cavort, cohort, consort, deport, distort,
distraught, escort, forecourt, forethought, onslaught,
passport, report, resort, spoilsport, support, transport

...ose
(e.g. rose)

1 Syllable

blows, bows, chose, close, clothes, crows, doze, flows,
toes, froze, glows, goes, grows, hose, knows, lows,
nose, pose, rose, rows, shows, slows, snows, sows,
those, throes, throws, toes, tows, woes

2 Syllables

arose, compose, depose, disclose, dispose, enclose,
expose, foreclose, impose, oppose, primrose, propose,
suppose, transpose

231

Intro

'a'

'e'

'i'

'o'

'u'

'tion'

Word
List

3 Syllables

decompose, UFOs

4 Syllables

lead by the nose, overexpose, superimpose,

under your nose

...ose

(e.g. dose)

1 Syllable

dose, close, gross

2 Syllables

engross, morose, verbose

...ose

(e.g. lose)

1 Syllable

blues, booze, bruise, chews, choose, clues, coups,
crews, cruise, cues, dews, fuse, hues, muse, news,
lose, ooze, queues, ruse, schmooze, screws, shoes,
skews, snooze, spews, use, views, whose, zoos

2 Syllables

abuse, accuse, amuse, bemuse, confuse, defuse,
diffuse, enthuse, excuse, infuse, misuse, refuse,
reuse, reviews, taboos, tattoos

3 Syllables

overuse, underuse

4 Syllables

radio news

Intro
'a'
'e'
'i'
'o'
'u'
'tion'
Word List

5 Syllables

electrical fuse, television news

...osed
(e.g. posed)

1 Syllable

closed, dozed, hosed, nosed

2 Syllables

composed, disclosed, disposed, enclosed, exposed,

imposed, opposed, proposed, supposed

3 Syllables

decomposed, juxtaposed, undisclosed, unopposed

4 Syllables

overexposed, superimposed

...osh

(e.g. posh)

see page 69 ...ash (e.g. wash)

...oss

(e.g. boss)

1 Syllable

boss, cross, doss, dross, floss, gloss, loss, moss,

sauce, toss

2 Syllables

across, backcross, big boss, chaos, crisscross, emboss,

ethos, kudos, lacrosse, pathos, uncross

Intro

'a'

'e'

'i'

'o'

'u'

'tion'

Word List

...ost
(e.g. lost)

1 Syllable
bossed, cost, crossed, flossed, frost, glossed,
lost, tossed

2 Syllables
accost, criss-crossed, defrost, embossed, exhaust,
riposte, uncrossed

...ost
(e.g. most)

see page 191 ...oast (e.g. boast)

...ot

(e.g. hot)

see also page 230 ...ort
(e.g. sport)

1 Syllable

blot, clot, cot, dot, got, hot, jot, knot, lot, not, plot, pot, rot, shot, slot, spot, squat, swat, tot, trot, watt

2 Syllables

a lot, bird shot, blind spot, blood clot, cannot, drop shot, dry rot, forgot, long shot, love knot, mug shot, must not, one shot, soft spot, weak spot, whole lot

3 Syllables

approach shot, melting pot, parking lot, passing shot, rifle shot, vacant lot

Intro

'a'

'e'

'i'

'o'

'u'

'tion'

Word List

...ote

(e.g. note)

see page 192 ...oat (e.g. boat)

...oth

(e.g. broth)

1 Syllable

cloth, broth, froth, goth, moth, sloth, wrath

...ouch

(e.g. pouch)

1 Syllable

couch, crouch, grouch, ouch, pouch, slouch, vouch

...ouch

(e.g. touch)

see page 255 ...uch (e.g. much)

Intro

'a'

'e'

'i'

'o'

'u'

'tion'

Word List

...oud

(e.g. loud)

1 Syllable

bowed, cloud, cowed, crowd, ploughed, proud, rowed, shroud, vowed, wowed

2 Syllables

allowed, aloud, avowed, dark-browed, dust cloud, endowed, miaowed, out loud, rain cloud, storm cloud, unbowed

3 Syllables

disallowed, overcrowd

Intro

...ough

(e.g. rough)

see page 258 ...uff (e.g. stuff)

'a'

'e'

...ould

(e.g. could)

see page 214 ...ood (e.g. wood)

'i'

'o'

'u'

'tion'

Word List

...ounce
(e.g. pounce)

1 Syllable
bounce, flounce, ounce, pounce, trounce

2 Syllables
announce, denounce, pronounce, renounce

3 Syllables
fluid ounce, mispronounce

...ound
(e.g. sound)

1 Syllable
bound, browned, crowned, downed, drowned,
found, frowned, ground, hound, mound, pound,
round, wound

Intro

'a'

'e'

'i'

'o'

'u'

'tion'

Word List

2 Syllables

around, astound, bring round, come round,
compound, confound, expound, gain ground,
impound, inbound, newfound, profound, propound,
pull round, rebound, renowned, resound, surround,
unbound, unsound, unwound

3 Syllables

common ground, drive around,
fool around, hang around, holy ground, lie around,
look around, play around, push around,
run aground, run around, turn around,
ultrasound, whirl around

4 Syllables

revolve around, sleeping around

6 Syllables

the other way around

Intro
'a'
'e'
'i'
'o'
'u'
'tion'
Word List

...ound

(e.g. war wound)

see page 220 ...ooned
(e.g. swooned)

...ouse

(e.g. house)

1 Syllable

house, louse, mouse, spouse

2 Syllables

boathouse, church mouse, doghouse,

dolls' house, jailhouse

...ove

(e.g. love)

1 Syllable

dove, glove, love, of, shove, guv, 've

2 Syllables

above, all of, kid glove, kind of, sort of

3 Syllables

boxing glove, hand and glove, hand in glove

Intro

'a'

'e'

'i'

'o'

'u'

'tion'

Word
List

...ove

(e.g. prove)

see also page 223 ...ooth (e.g. smooth)

1 Syllable

groove, move, prove, you've

2 Syllables

approve, disprove, improve, remove

3 Syllables

disapprove, on the move

4 Syllables

opening move

...OW
(e.g. now)

1 Syllable

bough, bow, brow, chow, cow, Frau, how, now, ow, plough, row, sow, vow, wow

2 Syllables

allow, and how, avow, cash cow, endow, kowtow, miaow, somehow

3 Syllables

disallow, sacred cow, take a bow

Intro

Intro

'a'

'e'

'i'

'o'

'u'

'tion'

Word
List

...ow

(e.g. blow)

see page 186 ...o (e.g. go)

...owed

(e.g. glowed)

see page 197 ...ode (e.g. rode)

...owed

(e.g. vowed)

see page 240 ...oud (e.g. loud)

...owl

(e.g. howl)

1 Syllable

cowl, foul, fowl, growl, howl, jowl, owl,

prowl, scowl

2 Syllables

afoul, night owl, towel

Intro
'a'
'e'
'i'
'o'
'u'
'tion'
Word List

...own

(e. g. clown)

1 Syllable

brown, clown, crown, drown, frown,

gown, town

Intro

'a'

2 Syllables

around, ball gown, boom town, downtown,
facedown, ghost town, half crown, renown, run-
down, small town, uptown

'e'

3 Syllables

bridal gown, triple crown, wedding gown

'i'

4 Syllables

talk of the town

'o'

...own
(e.g. blown)

'u'

see page 208 ...one (e.g. stone)

'tion'

Word List

...OX

(e.g. box)

1 Syllable

blocks, box, clocks, cocks, docks, flocks, fox, knocks,
locks, mocks, ox, rocks, shocks, socks, stocks

2 Syllables

outfox

Intro

'a'

'e'

'i'

'o'

'u'

'tion'

Word List

Intro

'a'

'e'

'i'

'o'

'u'

'tion'

Word List

...ub
(e.g. rub)

1 Syllable

bub, club, cub, drub, dub, grub, hub, nub, pub, rub, scrub, shrub, snub, stub, sub, tub

2 Syllables

bear cub, check stub, cheque stub

3 Syllables

lion cub, ticket stub, tiger cub

4 Syllables

flowering shrub, rotary club

...ube

(e.g. tube)

1 Syllable

boob, cube, lube, tube

2 Syllables

ice cube, stock cube

...uch

(e.g. much)

1 Syllable

clutch, crutch, dutch, hutch, much, such, touch

2 Syllables

as such, retouch, so much, too much

255

3 Syllables

a bit much, double dutch, rabbit hutch, very much

...uck

(e.g. struck)

1 Syllable

buck, chuck, duck, luck, muck, pluck, puck, ruck, schmuck, shuck, snuck, struck, stuck, suck, truck, tuck, yuck, yuk

2 Syllables

bad luck, get stuck, good luck, ill luck, lame duck, sound truck, unstuck

3 Syllables

garbage truck, pickup truck, run amok, sitting duck

5 Syllables

delivery truck

...ude

(e.g. rude)

see page 213 ...ood (e.g. mood)

...ue

(e.g. rue)

see page 210 ...oo (e.g. too)

Intro

'a'

'e'

'i'

'o'

'u'

'tion'

Word List

...uff

(e.g. stuff)

1 Syllable

bluff, buff, cuff, fluff, gruff, huff, muff, puff, rough,
ruff, scuff, snuff, stuff, tough

2 Syllables

enough, get tough, hot stuff, real stuff, rebuff

3 Syllables

good enough, in the buff, off the cuff, soon enough,
sure enough, well enough

4 Syllables

oddly enough, strangely enough

5 Syllables

create from raw stuff

6 Syllables
curiously enough

7 Syllables
interestingly enough

...ug
(e.g. bug)

1 Syllable
bug, drug, dug, hug, jug, lug, mug, plug, rug, shrug, slug, smug, snug, thug, tug

2 Syllables
bear hug, beer mug, debug, hard drug, soft drug, spark plug, unplug, wall plug

3 Syllables

coffee mug, scatter rug, water jug, wonder drug

4 Syllables

designer drug

5 Syllables

sweep under the rug

...uge
(e.g. huge)

1 Syllable

deluge, huge, refuge, rouge, Scrooge, stooge

...uilt

(e.g. guilt)

see page 156 ...ilt (e.g. tilt)

...uke

(e.g. fluke)

see also page 215 ...ook
(e.g. look)

1 Syllable

duke, fluke, gook, juke, kook, nuke, puke, rebuke,

sook, souk, spook

4 Syllables

gobbledygook

Intro

'a'

'e'

'i'

'o'

'u'

'tion'

Word List

...ule
(e.g. rule)

see page 217 ...ool (e.g. cool)

...ull
(e.g. pull)

1 Syllable
bull, full, pull, wool

2 Syllables
armful, artful, bowlful, brimful, chock-full, earful,
eyeful, fistful, handful, mouthful, plateful, push-pull,
roomful, spoonful, toadstool

...umb

(e.g. dumb)

see page 206 ...ome
(e.g. come)

...ume

(e.g. fume)

see page 218 ...oom
(e.g. room)

...ump
(e.g. bump)

1 Syllable

bump, chump, clump, dump, frump, grump, hump,
jump, lump, plump, pump, rump, slump, stump,
thump, trump

2 Syllables

high jump, long jump, tree stump

3 Syllables

garbage dump, rubbish dump, stomach pump,
water pump

4 Syllables

toxic waste dump

...un

(e.g. sun)

see also page 284 ...tion
(e.g. imagination)

1 Syllable

bun, done, fun, gun, none, one, pun, run, shun, son,
spun, stun, sun, ton, tonne, won

2 Syllables

begun, dry run, end run, fast one, home run, long
run, loved one, make fun, outdone, outrun, pension,
poke fun, redone, rerun, tension, undone

3 Syllables

ascension, attention, chicken run, contention,
convention, detention, dimension, extension,
invention, hired gun, machine gun, mother's son,
number one, one by one, overdone, pretension,
prevention, suspension

Intro

'a'

'e'

'i'

'o'

'u'

'tion'

Word
List

4 Syllables

apprehension, comprehension, condescension, favo(u)rite son, hypertension, in suspension, in the long run, not to mention, pay attention, reinvention

5 Syllables

misapprehension, paying attention

6 Syllables

centre of attention

...unch
(e.g. bunch)

1 Syllable

brunch, bunch, crunch, hunch, lunch, munch, punch, scrunch

2 Syllables

fruit punch

3 Syllables

credit crunch, knockout punch, rabbit punch

...und
(e.g. fund)

1 Syllable

fund, gunned, shunned, stunned, sunned

2 Syllables

fecund, outgunned, refund, rotund

...une

(e.g. tune)

see page 219 ...oon (e.g. moon)

...ung

(e.g. young)

1 Syllable

bung, hung, lung, rung, slung, sprung, strung, stung,

sung, swung, tongue, young

2 Syllables

among, unsung

3 Syllables

iron lung, mother tongue

4 Syllables

slip of the tongue

...unk

(e.g. drunk)

1 Syllable

bunk, chunk, clunk, drunk, dunk, flunk, funk, hunk,

junk, monk, plunk, punk, shrunk, skunk, spunk,

stunk, sunk, trunk

2 Syllables

debunk, tree trunk

Intro

'a'

'e'

'i'

'o'

'u'

'tion'

Word List

Intro

'a'

'e'

'i'

'o'

'u'

'tion'

Word List

...up
(e.g. up)

1 Syllable
cup, pup, sup, up

2 Syllables
close-up, egg cup

3 Syllables
coffee cup, golden cup, loving cup, painted cup,
paper cup

...ur
(e.g. fur)

see page 127 ...er (e.g. her)

...urb

(e.g. curb)

1 Syllable

blurb, curb, herb, kerb, verb

2 Syllables

disturb, reverb, superb

...ure

(e.g. pure)

see also page 80 ...aw (e.g. saw)

1 Syllable

cure, lure, pure, sure

Intro

'a'

'e'

'i'

'o'

'u'

'tion'

Word
List

2 Syllables

allure, brochure, couture, demure, endure, ensure, for sure, impure, insure, make sure, mature, obscure, secure, unsure

3 Syllables

haute couture, immature

4 Syllables

entrepreneur

...urge

(e.g. surge)

1 Syllable

dirge, merge, purge, scourge, splurge, surge, urge, verge

2 Syllables

converge, diverge, emerge, submerge

3 Syllables

re-emerge

4 Syllables

sexual urge

...url

(e.g. hurl)

1 Syllable

curl, earl, furl, girl, hurl, pearl, purl, swirl, twirl

2 Syllables

awhirl, cowgirl, newsgirl, playgirl, schoolgirl,
uncurl, unfurl

Intro

'a'

'e'

'i'

'o'

'u'

'tion'

Word List

...urld

(e.g. hurled)

1 Syllable

curled, hurled, swirled, twirled, whirled, world

2 Syllables

new world, unfurled

...urm

(e.g. sturm)

see page 172 ...irm (e.g. firm)

...urn
(e.g. burn)

1 Syllable

burn, churn, earn, learn, spurn, stern, turn,

urn, yearn

2 Syllables

adjourn, concern, discern, good turn, in turn,

return, upturn

3 Syllables

about turn, day return, in return

4 Syllables

without concern

5 Syllables

point of no return

Intro

'a'

'e'

'i'

'o'

'u'

'tion'

Word
List

...urt
(e.g. hurt)

1 Syllable

blurt, curt, dirt, flirt, hurt, pert, shirt, skirt, squirt

2 Syllables

alert, assert, concert, convert, divert, dress shirt, hair shirt, inert, insert, invert, pay dirt, pervert, revert, subvert, tee shirt, unhurt

3 Syllables

hit the dirt, reassert

...ush
(e.g. rush)

1 Syllable
blush, brush, crush, flush, gush, hush, lush, mush,
plush, rush, slush, thrush

3 Syllables
royal flush

...ush
(e.g. push)

1 Syllable
bush, cush, shush, tush, whoosh

Intro 'a' 'e' 'i' 'o' 'u' 'tion' Word List

Intro

'a'

'e'

'i'

'o'

'u'

'tion'

Word List

2 Syllables

ambush, bell-push, rose bush

3 Syllables

burning bush

...ust
(e.g. thrust)

1 Syllable

bussed, bust, crust, cussed, dust, fussed, gust, just, lust, rust, thrust, trust

2 Syllables

adjust, combust, discussed, disgust, distrust, encrust, entrust, gold dust, knife thrust, mistrust, nonplussed, robust, unjust

3 Syllables

angel dust, antitrust, cosmic dust, readjust

6 Syllables

radioactive dust

...ut

(e.g. cut)

1 Syllable

but, cut, glut, gut, hut, jut, mutt, nut, putt, rut, shut,

slut, smut, strut, tut, what

2 Syllables

all but, somewhat, uncut

Intro

'a'

'e'

'i'

'o'

'u'

'tion'

Word List

3 Syllables

rifle butt, water butt

4 Syllables

cigarette butt, kick in the butt

...ut
(e.g. put)

see page 222 ...oot (e.g. foot)

...utch

(e.g. crutch)

see page 255 ...uch (e.g. much)

...ute

(e.g. route)

see page 222 ...oot (e.g. root)

Intro

'a'

'e'

'i'

'o'

'u'

'tion'

Word List

Intro

'a'

'e'

'i'

'o'

'u'

'tion'

Word List

...tion
(e.g. imagination)

see also page 265
...un (e.g. sun)

2 Syllables

function, junction, mention, nation, pension,
ration, station, tension

3 Syllables

attention, bus station, carnation, castration, creation,
damnation, detention, dilation, dimension, donation,
duration, dysfunction, elation, extension, filtration,
fixation, flirtation, flotation, formation, foundation,
frustration, gas station, gestation, gradation, gyration,
inflation, injunction, invention, location, malfunction,
migration, mutation, narration, ovation, persuasion,
pretension, prevention, prostration, quotation, reflation,
relation, rotation, salvation, sedation, sensation,
stagnation, starvation, suspension, temptation, train
station, translation, vacation, vibration, vocation

Intro 'a' 'e' 'i' 'o' 'u' 'tion' Word List

4 Syllables

abdication, aberration, accusation, adaptation,

admiration, adoration, adulation, aggravation,

agitation, allegation, alteration, altercation,

amputation, animation, aspiration, automation,

blood relation, calculation, cancellation, celebration,

combination, compensation, complication,

concentration, condemnation, condensation,

condescension, confirmation, confiscation,

conflagration, confrontation, conservation,

consolation, constellation, consternation,

constipation, consultation, consummation,

contemplation, conversation, coronation,

cultivation, declaration, decoration, dedication,

degradation, delegation, demonstration,

deportation, deprivation, desecration, designation,

desolation, desperation, destination, detonation,

devastation, deviation, dislocation, domination,

duplication, education, emigration, emulation,

escalation, evocation, excavation, excitation,

Intro

'a'

'e'

'i'

'o'

'u'

'tion'

Word List

Intro

'a'

'e'

'i'

'o'

'u'

'tion'

Word
List

exclamation, exhalation, expectation, explanation,
exploitation, exploration, fabrication, fascination,
fragmentation, generation, hesitation, illustration,
imitation, immigration, implication, impregnation,
imputation, incantation, incarnation, inclination,
incubation, indication, indignation, infestation,
infiltration, inflammation, information, innovation,
inspiration, installation, integration, intimation,
invitation, invocation, irritation, isolation,
jubilation, laceration, legislation, liberation,
lubrication, machination, masturbation,
medication, meditation, molestation, motivation,
mutilation, navigation, obligation, observation,
occupation, ostentation, penetration, perspiration,
petrol station, police station, power station,
preparation, preservation, proclamation,
protestation, provocation, publication, punctuation,
radiation, railroad station, railway station,
realization, recantation, recreation, relaxation,
reputation, reservation, resignation, respiration,
restoration, revelation, saturation, segregation,

separation, service station, simulation, situation, speculation, stimulation, stipulation, strangulation, subway station, suffocation, taste sensation, termination, titillation, toleration, touch sensation, transformation, transportation, trepidation, tribulation, tv station, vegetation, vindication, violation

5 Syllables

abomination, acceleration, accommodation, across the nation, administration, african nation, alienation, amalgamation, annihilation, articulation, assassination, assimilation, authentication, authorization, civilization, collaboration, communication, confederation, configuration, conglomeration, congratulation, consideration, contamination, cooperation, decapitation, deceleration, degeneration, deification, demonization, denunciation, depreciation, determination, detoxication, discrimination, disinformation, disintegration,

Intro

'a'

'e'

'i'

'o'

'u'

'tion'

Word
List

ejaculation, elaboration, elimination,
emancipation, equivocation, eradication,
evacuation, evaluation, evaporation,
exacerbation, exaggeration, examination,
exasperation, exhilaration, extermination,
fortification, glorification, gratification,
hallucination, humiliation, illumination,
imagination, immunization, impersonation,
improvisation, incarceration, incrimination,
indoctrination, infatuation, initiation,
insemination, insinuation, instrumentation,
interpretation, interrogation, intimidation,
intoxication, investigation, in operation, job
application, justification, magnification,
manifestation, manipulation, misapprehension,
miscalculation, misinformation, negotiation,
notification, optimization, organization,
orientation, ornamentation, participation,
pontification, precipitation, predestination,
premeditation, privatization, procrastination,
proliferation, purification, qualification, radio

station, ramification, recommendation, recrimination, regeneration, reincarnation, rejuvenation, representation, retaliation, reverberation, sanctification, simplification, standing ovation, sterilization, verification, victimization, visualization

6 Syllables

cannibalization, capitalization, centre of attention, criminalization, decontamination, detoxification, hono(u)rable mention, hospitalization, identification, miscommunication, misinterpretation, misrepresentation, renegotiation, self-congratulation, self-determination, sexual relation

7 Syllables

suspended animation, victory celebration

8 Syllables

artificial respiration, character assassination, confidential information, institutionalization

Intro

'a'

'e'

'i'

'o'

'u'

'tion'

Word List

Intro

'a'

'e'

'i'

'o'

'u'

'tion'

Word
List

Intro

'a'

'e'

'i'

'o'

'u'

'tion'

Word List

admiration 285
admire 171
admission fee 108
admit 177
ado 210
adoration 285
adore 81
adorn 229
adrift 150
adulation 285
advance 51
advertising
  campaign 37
advice 140
advise 174
Aegean sea 108
afar 59
affair 38
affect 102
affirm 172
afire 171
aflame 48
afloat 192
aflutter 127
afoul 249
afraid 31
afresh 130
african nation 287
afternoon 219
afternoon tea 108

again 36, 120
again and
  again 121
against the
  clock 195
age 35
age norm 228
aged 143
aggravation 285
aggrieve 101
aghast 72
agile 154
agitation 285
ago 186
agree 105
agreed 109
agreed upon 208
ahead 104
aid 30
aide 30
ail 41
aim 48
ain't 39
air 38
air attack 27
air base 24
air mail 41
air raid 31
air wave 79
airport 231

airy 105
ajar 59
alarm 64
alarm clock 195
alas 71
ale 41
alert 276
alienation 287
alight 179
align 162
aligned 160
alike 152
alive 182
all 43
all along 209
all but 279
all clear 93
all in all 44
all of 245
all the same 48
all the while 154
all told 201
all too 210
allayed 31
allegation 285
alley 105
alley cat 74
allied 145
allies 174
allow 247

allowed 240
allude 213
allure 272
ally 147
alm 205
alone 208
along 209
alongside 146
aloof 215
aloud 240
alright 179
alteration 285
altercation 285
although 186
am 47
amalgamation
    287
amass 71
amassed 72
ambush 278
amen 120
amend 122
amid 143
amiss 175
among 268
amp 49
amply 105
amputation 285
amuse 233

amusement
    park 63
an 50
and 52
and co. 186
and how 247
and I 147
and so 186
and that 74
and they 83
and to 210
and you 210
anew 210
angel cake 40
angel dust 279
angel food
    cake 40
angle of view 212
angry 105
animal skin 159
animation 285
annihilation 287
announce 242
anoint 200
antitank 55
antitrust 279
antsy 105
any 105
any hour 128
anymore 81

apace 24
apart 67
ape 57
aplomb 205
app 56
appall 44
appeal 110
appealed 111
appear 93
appeared 95
appease 97
append 122
apple pie 147
applied 145
applies 174
apply 147
appoint 200
apprehend 123
apprehension 266
approach 187
approach shot 237
approve 246
apron string 164
apt 58, 126
arc 62
arc light 179
arcade 31
arcane 36
are 59
arid 143

Intro

'a'

'e'

'i'

'o'

'u'

'tion'

Word
List

Intro

'a'

'e'

'i'

'o'

'u'

'tion'

Word
List

Intro

'a'

'e'

'i'

'o'

'u'

'tion'

Word
List

begat 74
begin 159
beguile 154
beguiled 153
begun 265
behalf 32
behave 79
behind 160
behind bars 66
behold 201
Beijing 164
Beirut 222
believe 101
bell 117
bell jar 59
belle 117
belle vue 210
bell-push 278
belong 209
below 186
belt 118
bemoan 208
bemuse 233
bench 121
bench mark 62
bend 122
bend your ear 94
beneath 100
benign 162
bent 124

bequeath 100
bequest 132
bequests 131
berate 76
bereave 101
berk 128
berry 106
berserk 128
beset 135
beside 145
best 132
best friend 122
best man 50
bet 134
betray 83
betrayed 31
between 112
beware 38
bewitch 141
beyond control
    203
beyond the
    sea 108
bible belt 119
bicker 127
bicycle wheel 110
bid 143
bide 145
biding 164
big 151

big band 52
big ben 120
big game 48
big top 224
big wheel 110
bike 152
bill 155
bill of sale 41
bill sticker 127
billionaire 38
bin 159
bind 160
binned 166
bioengineer 94
bird 170
bird of prey 84
bird shot 237
birdbath 77
bird's eye 147
bird's nest 132
birr 127
birth control 203
birth rate 76
birthday suit 222
bit 177
bit by bit 177
bit part 67
bitch 141
bitchy 106
bite 179

bitsy 106
bitter end 123
bivalve 46
bizarre 59
blab 22
black 26
black and
    white 180
black belt 119
black eye 147
black sheep 114
black tie 147
blacked 28
blackly 106
blade 30
blagg 34
blame 48
bland 52
blandly 106
blank 55
blank shell 118
blank space 24
blankly 106
blare 38
blast 72
bleach 89
bleakly 106
bleary 106
bled 104
bleed 108

bleeding heart 67
bleep 113
blend 122
bless 131
blessed 132
blew 210
blick 142
blight 179
blighted 143
blind 160
blind date 76
blind man 50
blind spot 237
blinded 143
blindly 106
bling 164
blink 165
blink of an eye 148
bliss 175
blithely 106
bloat 192
blob 193
block 194
blockade 31
blocks 251
bloke 188
blood bank 55
blood cell 118
blood clot 237
blood disease 97

blood feud 213
blood line 162
blood relation 285
blood test 132
blood type 169
bloodbath 77
bloody 106
bloody shame 48
bloom 218
blot 237
blow 186
blow fly 147
blowed 197
blown 208
blows 231
blowsy 106
blowy 106
blowzy 106
blue 210
blue sky 147
blue whale 41
blues 233
bluff 258
bluntly 106
blur 127
blurb 271
blurred 170
blurry 106
blurt 276
blush 277

Intro

'a'

'e'

'i'

'o'

'u'

'tion'

Word
List

brush aside 146

brute 222

bub 254

bubble gum 207

bubble wrap 56

bubbly 106

buck 256

buddy 106

buff 258

buffet 83

buffoon 219

bug 259

building block 195

building site 180

built 156

bull 262

bulletproof vest
133

bull's eye 147

bum 206

bump 264

bump into 212

bumpy 106

bun 265

bunch 266

bung 268

bunk 269

bunny 106

burglar alarm 64

burial site 180

burial vault 45

burly 106

burn 275

burn mark 62

burning bush 278

bury 106

bus fare 38

bus route 222

bus station 284

bus stop 224

bush 277

business deal 110

business suit 222

busload 198

bussed 278

bust 278

busty 106

busy 106

busy bee 108

but 279

but I 147

butt end 122

butter 127

buy 146

buy into 212

buyer 171

buys 174

by 146

by and by 147

by chance 51

by design 162

by hook or by
crook 216

by the bye 147

by the way 84

bye 146

bye-bye 147

C

C.I.A. 84

C.D. 106

C.E.O. 186

cab 22

cab fare 38

cabaret 84

cable car 59

cache 68

cad 29

cadet 135

café 83

caffeine 112

cage 35

cagey 106

cajole 202

cajoled 201

cake 40

calculation 285

calf 32

call 43

Intro

'a'

'e'

'i'

'o'

'u'

'tion'

Word List

Intro

'a'

'e'

'i'

'o'

'u'

'tion'

Intro

'a'

'e'

'i'

'o'

'u'

'tion'

Word List

Intro

'a'

'e'

'i'

'o'

'u'

'tion'

Word List

Intro

'a'

'e'

'i'

'o'

'u'

'tion'

Word List

Intro

'a'

'e'

'i'

'o'

'u'

'tion'

Word List

first class 60, 71
first grade 31
first light 179
first of all 44
firstborn 229
firsthand 53
firstly 106
fiscal year 94
fish steak 40
fish wife 149
fishing gear 94
fishing net 135
fist 176
fistful 262
fit 177
five 181
fix 182
fixation 284
flab 22
flack 26
flag 34
flail 41
flair 38
flake 40
flame 48
flan 50
flank 55
flap 56
flapped 58, 126
flare 38

flash 68
flash point 200
flask 70
flat 74
flaw 80
flay 83
flayed 30
flea 105
fleas 97
fledge 105
flee 105
fleece 88
fleet 99
flesh 130
fleur 127
flew 210
flick 142
flicker 127
flicks 182
flier 171
flies 174
flight 179
fling 164
flint 167
flip 168
flirt 276
flirtation 284
flirty 106
flit 177
flitted 143

float 192
flock 194
flocks 251
floor 80
floor show 186
floozy 106
flop 224
floss 235
flossed 236
flotation 284
flounce 242
flow 186
flow from 205, 206
flowed 197
flower 127
flower stalk 43
flowering shrub 254
flown 208
flows 231
flu 210
flue 210
fluff 258
fluid 143
fluid ounce 242
fluke 261
flunk 269
flush 277
flute 222

H

Intro

'a'

'e'

'i'

'o'

'u'

'tion'

Word List

hair spray 83
hair style 154
half 32
half crown 250
half track 27
halfway 83
hall 43
hall of fame 48
hallowe'en 113
hallucination 288
halt 45
halve 68
ham 47
hand 52
hand and glove 245
hand brake 40
hand grenade 31
hand in glove 245
hand job 193
handful 262
handheld 116
handmade 31
hang 54
hang around 243
hang glide 145
happy 107
happy chance 52
happy event 124
harangue 54

harass 71
harassed 72
hard 61
hard drink 165
hard drug 259
hard liquor 127
hard sell 118
hard to please 97
hardcore 81
harm 64
harp 65
harpoon 219
harpooned 220
hart 67
has been 159
hash 68
haste 73
hasty 107
hat 74
hatch 75
hatchet job 193
hatchet man 50
hate 76
hated 144
haul 43
haul away 84
haute couture 272
have 80
have a go at it 178
have been 159

have in
  mind 160
have to 211
have to
  have 80
have you 211
hawk 42
hay 83
hay bale 41
hazy 107
he 105
head 104
head ache 40
head game 48
head start 67
headroom 218
heady 107
heal 109
healed 111
health 91
healthy 107
heap 113
hear 93
heard 170
hearing aid 31
heart 67
heart and soul
  203
heart attack 27
heart disease 97

Intro

'a'

'e'

'i'

'o'

'u'

'tion'

Word List

L

L.A.P.D. 108
L.P. 107
lab 22
lace 24
laced 73
laceration 286
lack 26
lacked 28
lacks 82
lacrosse 235
lacy 107
lad 29
ladies' man 50
lady 107
lady friend 123
lag 34
lagoon 219
laid 30
laid low 186
lain 36
lair 38
laissez faire 38
lake 40
lamb 47
lame 48
lame duck 256
lament 124
lamp 49

lamp shade 31
land 52
land mine 162
land site 179
landing strip 168
lane 36
languid 144
lap 56
lapped 58
lapped 126
lard 61
largesse 131
lark 62
laser beam 92
lash 68
lass 71
last 72
last frontier 94
latch 75
late 76
lathe 78
laugh 32
laugh at 74
launch pad 30
laundry 107
law 81
lawn 207, 229
lax 82
lay 83
lay aside 146

lay claim 48
lay into 212
lay to rest 133
lay waste to 212
laying claim 48
lazy 107
lead 104, 108
lead astray 84
lead by the
    nose 232
leading light 180
lean 112
leap 113
leap year 93
leaped 126
leapt 126
learn 275
lease 88
leave 101
leave behind 160
lech 136
led 104
ledge 105
leech 89
leer 93
left brain 36
left wing 164
leg it 177
legal right 180
legal transfer 128

Intro 'a' 'e' 'i' 'o' 'u' 'tion' Word List

Intro

'a'

'e'

'i'

'o'

'u'

'tion'

Word List

Intro
'a'
'e'
'i'
'o'
'u'
'tion'
Word List

Intro
'a'
'e'
'i'
'o'
'u'
'tion'
Word List

overfed 104
overfeed 109
overflow 186
overflowed 198
overgrown 209
overhead 104
overhear 94
overheard 170
overnight 180
overnight bag 34
overnight case 25
overpaid 31
overplay 84
overplayed 31
overprotect 103
overran 50
overreact 29
overripe 169
overseas 97
oversize 174
overslept 126
oversold 202
overspent 124
overspill 155
overstay 84
overstayed 31
overthrew 212
overthrown 209
overtook 216
overtrain 37

overuse 233
overweight 76
overwork 128
overwrite 180
ow 247
owe 186
owed 197
owl 249
own 208
ox 251
oxygen mask 70

P

p.m. 119
pace 24
paced 73
pack 26
pack rat 74
packed 28
packhorse 230
packing case 25
packs 82
pact 28
pacts 82
pad 29
page 35
paid 30
pail 41
pain 36

pain in the arse 60
pain in the ass 71
paint 39
painted 144
painted cup 270
pair 38
pale 41
pall 43
palm 64, 205
pan 50
panache 68
pane 36
panic attack 27
panned 52
pansy 107
pantry 107
paper bag 34
paper chase 25
paper cup 270
par 59
parade 31
parallel bars 66
park 62
parking lot 237
parking space 25
parlo(u)r game 48
parole 202
paroled 201

Intro

'a'

'e'

'i'

'o'

'u'

'tion'

Word List

Intro

'a'

'e'

'i'

'o'

'u'

'tion'

Word List

put through 211
put to sleep 114
putt 279

Q

quack 26
quacks 82
quaint 39
quake 40
qualification 288
quash 69
quay 105
Queen 112
Queen of the
  night 180
quell 117
quelled 116
quench 121
question mark 63
questionnaire 38
queue 210
queues 233
quick 142
quicker 127
quid 143
quid pro quo 186
quilt 156
quip 168
quirk 128

quirky 107
quit 177
quite 179
quotation 284
quote 192

R

R.A.M. 47
rabbi 147
rabbit hutch 256
rabbit punch 267
race 24
racecourse 230
raced 73
racehorse 230
racer 127
racing car 59
rack 26
rack of lamb 47
racked 28
racketeer 94
racks 82
radiation 286
radio news 233
radio station 288
radio wave 79
radioactive dust
  279
rag 34

rage 35
ragged 144
ragu 211
raid 30
rail 41
railroad car 59
railroad station
  286
railroad track 27
railway car 59
railway station 286
railway yard 61
rain 36
rain cloud 240
rainy 107
rainy day 84
raise 85
rake 40
ram 47
ramification
  288
ran 50
rang 54
rank 55
rank and file 154
rap 56
rape 57
rapid 144
rapid climb 158
rapped 58

Intro

'a'

'e'

'i'

'o'

'u'

'tion'

Word List

Intro
'a'
'e'
'i'
'o'
'u'
'tion'
Word List

Intro

'a'

'e'

'i'

'o'

'u'

'tion'

Word List

scotland yard 61
scourge 272
scowl 249
scrap 56
scrape 57
scrape by 147
scrapped 58
scrapped 126
scratch 75
scratch pad 30
scrawl 43
scream 92
screech 89
screen 112
screen test 133
screw 210
screwed 213
screws 233
scroll 202
Scrooge 260
scrub 254
scrunch 266
scuff 258
sculpted 144
scum 206
sea 105
sea breeze 97
sea spray 83
seahorse 230
seal 109

sealed 111
seam 92
sear 93
seared 95
seas 97
seat 99
seat belt 119
seclude 213
second class 60
second class 71
second hand 53
second sight 180
secret code 198
secret plan 50
secret police 89
sect 102
secure 272
sedan 50
sedate 76
sedation 284
seduce 221
see 105
see eye to eye 148
see through 211
see to it 177
seed 108
seeing red 104
seem 92
seen 112
seep 113

sees 97
segment 124
segregation 286
seize 97
select 102
self 117
self-congratulation 289
self-control 203
self-determination 289
self-professed 133
sell 117
send 122
señor 81
sensation 284
sensationalize 174
sense of right and wrong 210
sense of shame 49
sense of smell 118
sense of taste 73
sent 124
sentry 107
separation 287
sequin 159
sequinned 166
serenade 31
serene 112

Intro

'a'

'e'

'i'

'o'

'u'

'tion'

Word List

Intro

'a'

'e'

'i'

'o'

'u'

'tion'

Word List

Intro

'a'

'e'

'i'

'o'

'u'

'tion'

Word
List

stepped 126
sterilization 289
stern 275
stew 210
stewed 213
stick 142
stick by 147
stick to 211
sticker 127
sticks 182
stiffed 150
stile 154
stiletto heel 110
still 155
stillborn 229
stimulation 287
sting 164
stink 165
stint 167
stipulation 287
stir 127
stir fry 147
stirred 170
stitch 141
stock 194
stock cube 255
stock list 176
stocks 251
stoke 188
stole 202

stomach ache 40
stomach flu 212
stomach pump
  264
stomach upset
  135
stone 208
stone age 35
stony 107
stood 214
stooge 260
stool 217
stoop to 211
stop 224
stop dead 104
storage device
  140
storage space 25
store 81
stork 42
storm 228
storm cloud 240
stormy 107
story 107
stowed 197
straight 76
straight line 162
strain 36
strait 76
strand 52

strangely enough
  258
strangulation 287
strap 56
strapped 58
strapped 126
straw 81
straw man 50
strawberry jam 47
stray 83
strayed 30
stream 92
street 99
street sign 162
stress 131
stressed 132
stretch 136
stretch mark 62
strewn 219
stride 145
strider 127
striding 164
strife 149
strike 152
strike hard 61
string 164
string along 209
strip 168
strip show 186
stripe 169

Intro

'a'

'e'

'i'

'o'

'u'

'tion'

Word List

Intro
'a'
'e'
'i'
'o'
'u'
'tion'
Word List

thick skin 159
thicker 127
thigh 146
thighs 174
thing 164
think 165
think twice 140
thirsty 107
this 175
this night 179
thong 209
thorn 229
thorny 107
those 231
though 186
thought 230
thrall 43
thrash 68
thread 104
threat 134
three 105
threes 97
threw 210
thrift 150
thrill 155
thrive 181
throat 192
throb 193
throes 231
throne 208

throng 209
through 210
through and
    through 212
throw 186
throw a fit 177
throw away 84
thrown 208
throws 231
thru 210
thrush 277
thrust 278
thug 259
thumb 206
thump 264
thyme 158
tick 142
ticker 127
ticker tape 57
ticket stub 254
ticks 182
tics 182
tidal flow 186
tidal wave 79
tide 145
tidy 107
tie 146
tie rack 27
tied 145
ties 174

tiger cub 254
tight 179
tightend 122
tightly 107
tightrope 225
tile 154
tiled 153
till 155
tilt 156
Timbuktu 212
time 158
time and again
    121
time and time
    again 121
time lag 34
time machine 113
time of day 84
time out of mind
    161
time to go 186
time to grieve 101
Times Square 38
timid 144
tin 159
tin can 50
tin foil 199
tingly 107
tinned 166
tint 167

Intro

'a'

'e'

'i'

'o'

'u'

'tion'

Word List

Intro

'a'

'e'

'i'

'o'

'u'

'tion'

Word List

wash 69
wash away 84
washing day 84
waste 73
waste pipe 169
wasted 144
wasting away 84
water butt 280
water gap 56
water jug 260
water line 163
water pipe 169
water pump 264
water rat 74
water right 180
water sprite 180
water tap 56
water wheel 110
watt 237
wave 79
wax 82
way 83
we 105
weak part 67
weak point 200
weak spot 237
wealth 91
wealthy man 50
wean 112
wear 38

wear and tear 38
wear away 84
weary 107
weasel word 170
weather map 56
weather vane 37
weave 101
wed 104
we'd 108
wedding band 53
wedding cake 40
wedding day 84
wedding dress 131
wedding gift 151
wedding gown 250
wedding night 180
wedding ring 164
wedge 105
weed 108
weep 113
weigh 83
weighed 30
weight 76
welcome mat 74
weld 116
well 117
we'll 109, 155
well enough 258
well known 208
welt 118

wench 121
wend 122
went 124
wept 126
we're 93
were 127
west 132
West End 122
West Side 145
wet 134
we've 101
whack 26
whacked 28
whacks 82
whale 41
wham 47
what 279
what a mess 131
what are they 84
what are you 212
what did 144
what did you 212
what do you 212
what for 81
what you're 81
wheat 99
wheel 109
wheeled 111
wheeze 97
when 120

when 159
where 38
whet 134
whew 210
whey 83
which 141
Whig 151
while 154
while away 84
whim 157
whimsy 107
whine 162
whip 168
whip hand 53
whip through 211
whirl around 243
whirled 274
whisky 107
whispering
    campaign 37
whistle stop 225
whit 177
white 179
white gold 201
white heat 99
white knight 179
white shark 62
white trash 68
white whale 41
whitewash 69

who 210
whoa 186
who'd 213
whole 202
whole lot 237
whole note 192
whole thing 164
who'll 217
whom 218
whoosh 277
whore 81
whose 233
why 146
wick 142
wicked 144
wicked witch 141
wicks 182
wide 145
wide of the mark 63
wide screen 112
wider 127
widespread 104
wield 111
wierd 95
wife 149
wig 151
wild 153
wild man 50
wild thyme 158
Wild West 133

wildly 107
wile 154
wiled 153
will 155
willful neglect 103
wilt 156
wilted 144
win 159
wind 160, 166
wind scale 41
winded 144
window frame 49
window sash 69
window shade 31
windy 107
wine 162
wine and dine
    163
wined 160
wing 164
wink 165
wink at 74
winning post 191
wipe 169
wipe away 84
wiper blade 31
wire 171
wire cutter 128
wise 174
wise guy 147

Intro
'a'
'e'
'i'
'o'
'u'
'tion'
Word List

Intro

'a'

'e'

'i'

'o'

'u'

'tion'

Word List

Further Resources

Use this book as a companion to the following titles in the same series.

How to Write Great Songs, Michael Heatley & Alan Brown
(Flame Tree Publishing 2007). Hundreds of examples from 100 great
rock and pop songwriters.

Guitar Chords, edited by Jake Jackson, (Flame Tree Publishing, 2006)
All the basic guitar chords in a single handy format: easy to play and read.

Piano Chords, edited by Jake Jackson, (Flame Tree Publishing, 2007)
All the basic Piano chords. Great for rock, pop and jazz music.

How to Read Music, Alan Charlton (Flame Tree Publishing, 2008)
A comprehensive introduction to music in a pocket sized format.

Available from your local bookstore, Amazon or direct from the Publisher
online at *www.flametreepublishing.com*

Other good books in this area include:

Sammy Cahn's Rhyming Dictionary. Sammy Cahn (Cherry Lane Music, 2002)
A classic, quirky, clever book by a master songwriter.

All You Need is Ears. George Martin. (St Martins Press, 1995)
The brilliant Beatles producer gives his take on writing and producing music.

The Music of Joni Mitchell. Lloyd Whitesell. (OUP, 2008)
An excellent insight into the techniques and inspirations of a top songwriter.

**There are numerous ryhming dictionaries on the internet, but care is
needed when using them because most generate thousands of random
non-words as well as more formal and poetic words.**